Unmasking the Jezebel Spirit

ENDORSEMENTS

Every pastor should read with discernment this very important book. With direction from the Holy Spirit, the information in *Unmasking the Jezebel Spirit* could save us some unnecessary heartache and trials.

Ché Ahn

Senior Pastor, Harvest Rock Church, Pasadena, California

The Jezebel spirit is real and can cause great havoc in a church or an individual. In *Unmasking the Jezebel Spirit*, John Paul Jackson draws from biblical insights, coupled with examples, as he handles this delicate subject with wisdom and clarity.

Elizabeth (Beth) Alves

President, Intercessors International

Will the real Jezebel please stand up! When Christians throw the kitchen sink at each other and one of them is a woman, you may hear the phrase, "She has a Jezebel spirit." The demon who reigned in Queen Jezebel loves it! If you're on his to do list, he won't want you to read *Unmasking the Jezebel Spirit*.

Harald Bredesen

Chairman, The Prince of Peace Foundation

Do you enjoy being flattered? Watch out! Convinced nobody could ever manipulate you? Take care! Attracted by anointing and gifting? Tread wisely! You may already be a target by this spirit, particularly if you are in a leadership position. Written wisely but purposefully, *Unmasking the Jezebel Spirit* could save you years of heartache and eventual destruction.

Gerald Coates

Speaker, Author, and Broadcaster, United Kingdom

The attack against prophetic ministry is ongoing and merciless. Weak Ahab leadership, controlled by an intimidating Jezebel spirit, strikes at the very foundation of the Church. Speaking with wisdom, faith, and calm authority, John Paul Jackson pinpoints exactly where the enemy is operating. Not reading *Unmasking the Jezebel Spirit* will allow the enemy to remain undetected. I loved this book!

GRAHAM COOKE

Author of *Developing Your Prophetic Gift*

This teaching in *Unmasking the Jezebel Spirit* is very much needed by the Church. I am grateful John Paul Jackson is able to clearly expose how the Jezebel spirit works. This book will help leaders be on their guard, and then handle the issues raised in a godly way.

DAVID A. DEVENISH

Author of *Demolishing Strongholds*

Unmasking the Jezebel Spirit is a word in due season that sheds light, understanding, and wisdom on this destructive and diabolical spirit. Every leader and emerging leader must read this book. It will assist you in tracking and detecting when your ministry is about to come under siege.

AARON EVANS

Vice President, Streams Ministries International

John Paul Jackson gives practical insights on detecting the enemy at work through deceit, manipulation, and control. He gives wise counsel and real-life situations of what can happen to an undiscerning pastor or church leadership. I could have avoided some pitfalls if I'd had this awareness thirty years ago.

DON FINTO

Founder, The Caleb Company

Lurking behind the scenes of many disasters in the Church today is the Jezebel spirit. With the boldness of prophets who have gone before him, John Paul Jackson unmasks this veiled ploy and releases a laser beam of light to dispel darkness and declare truth. Warning: *Unmasking the Jezebel Spirit* will arm you for the battle of the millennium!

JIM W. GOLL

Founder, Ministry to the Nations

Author of *The Lost Art of Intercession* and *Father Forgive Us!*

A timely and helpful book from John Paul Jackson's years of observation. As God's Church is often oblivious to Satan's devices, *Unmasking the Jezebel Spirit* is an excellent exposé. It raises awareness about the enemy's intrigues and alerts leaders to the spiritual battles facing them.

BRIAN HAYES
Senior Pastor, Edinburgh City Fellowship, Scotland

Unmasking the Jezebel Spirit should be a great help to leadership. It identifies the Jezebel spirit, and also outlines valuable principles in setting "sheep" free who have been subjected to this spirit's dominating and crippling effect. This evil opposition must be overcome if the Church is to become all God has called her to become.

BOB JONES
Bob Jones Ministries

Every pastor and every layperson should read *Unmasking the Jezebel Spirit*. It could save their church or ministry.

DR. R. T. KENDALL
Former Senior Pastor, Westminster Chapel, London, England

John Paul Jackson once again shoots straight from the hip in exposing this very divisive spirit. It is imperative that the Body of Christ recognize and deal in a scriptural manner with this important subject. A must-read for those in leadership!

JONI LAMB
Television Host, Daystar Television Network

For too long the Church has swung to extremes regarding the Jezebel spirit: either outright denial or hysterical overreaction. Finally, this terrible force has been drawn out into the cold, dear light for exposure, inspection, and execution. *Unmasking the Jezebel Spirit* is a ground-breaking, turf-taking foray against Satan's wiles.

JOHN L. MOORE
Author of *The Breaking of Ezra Riley*

Unmasking the Jezebel Spirit is a deadly weapon to be used against the enemy. John Paul Jackson has provided valuable insights into the enemy's schemes. Treat this book with the respect it deserves.

David Ravenhill

Author of *They Drank From the River and Died in the Wilderness*

I am personally gratified that John Paul Jackson's teaching on the Jezebel spirit has taken printed form. *Unmasking the Jezebel Spirit* is easily readable, skillfully balanced, cautiously presented, and more desperately needed than ever before. I highly recommend it.

Jack Taylor

President, Dimensions Ministries, Melbourne, Florida

John Paul Jackson has done a very thorough and effective job in blowing the whistle on the Jezebel spirit as it operates in the Church today. I agree with all he says in *Unmasking the Jezebel Spirit.*

Doris M. Wagner

Executive Vice President, Global Harvest Ministries,
Colorado Springs, Colorado

John Paul Jackson

Unmasking the Jezebel Spirit

Previously titled
The Veiled Ploy

Foreword by
Lou Engle

Requests for information should be addressed to:
Streams Publishing House
4004 Gateway Dr. Ste 100
Colleyville, TX 76034
www.streamsministries.com

ISBN 1-58483-049-2

Printed on acid-free paper in the USA.

To the hundreds of pastors
who have shared their stories,
to the many prophetic voices who have
been silenced at the hands of this spirit,
to the intercessors who have been
crushed under the weight of this
oppressive foe; may you find
healing from the pain.

To those who have
succumbed to this spirit
and recovered, may your gifts
one day be used to
further the glorious
Kingdom of God.

Also by John Paul Jackson

7 Days Behind the Veil: Throne Room Meditations
Breaking Free of Rejection
I AM Youth Curriculum
I AM: Inheriting the Fullness of God's Names
I AM: 365 Names of God
Moments with God Dream Journal
Buying and Selling the Souls of Our Children
Needless Casualties of War

Foreword By
LOU ENGLE

THERE ARE MOMENTS IN history when a door for massive change opens. Great revolutions for good or for evil occur in the vacuum created by these openings. It is in these times that key men and women, even entire generations, risk everything to become the hinge of history—the pivotal point to determine which way the door will swing.

Elijah was such a man. Born into one of the darkest times of Israel's history, his calling in life was literally to turn an entire nation back to God. At that time, King Ahab and his heathen wife, Jezebel, seemed to be on a personal mission from hell to stamp out the righteousness that remained in Israel. They served the vile Canaanite idols, Baal and Ashtoreth, demonic principalities that demanded sexual immorality and perversion in their fertility rituals. In her rampage, Jezebel built pagan altars and murdered the Lord's prophets, replacing them with more than 800 occult priests, soothsayers, and temple prostitutes. Israel, a nation belonging to the Lord, sunk into its deepest moral morass.

The influence of demonic power operating through Jezebel was so great that out of 10 million Israelites, only 7,000 were considered faithful to the Lord. Jezebel influenced them to forsake their covenant with God. She was responsible for corrupting an entire nation. In the midst of this spiritual seduction, Elijah strode onto the scene to confront Ahab, Jezebel, and their legions of pagan sorcerers. In the midst of unspeakable depravity, Elijah stood as a solitary voice for righteousness. This holy man was God's answer to the cohorts of hell hosted by Jezebel!

America is much like Israel of that day. Our nation was founded on God's laws by our righteous forefathers. Now we see the same spirit of Jezebel rising to destroy every vestige of godly heritage.

Years ago a woman in our church in Pasadena, California had a dream where she was crying out, "I see Elijah." The entire congregation began to chant, "Elijah, Elijah, Elijah." As they were chanting, a white cross appeared on a blue curtain in the church. The congregation's chant turned into, "Jesus, Jesus, Jesus." Suddenly a mighty rushing wind swept through the auditorium.

When the woman shared her dream with the pastoral staff, we wrote to some prophetic friends seeking an understanding of the dream. The consensus was, clearly there was coming a prophetic Elijah movement that would bring an unveiling of the Cross and help to usher in a mighty wind of revival. Chris Berglund, a friend of mine, took the woman's dream and prayed, "God, if there's more to this dream, give me insight." That night Chris dreamed the exact same dream, but at the end of the dream he heard a voice say, "That which hinders Elijah is Jezebel."

Today, there is mortal combat in this nation between the spirit of Elijah and the spirit of Jezebel. The contenders on both sides are the prophets. To the victor goes the soul of the nation. Jezebel's greatest fear and archenemies are the prophets, for they expose her schemes and call the Church to repentance.

John Paul Jackson is a prophetic father who, in the spirit of Elijah, is exposing Jezebel's activity. *Unmasking the Jezebel Spirit* is a voice calling us to a "no toleration" mentality in our lives and in our churches. While reading it, I found the Spirit of God deeply probing me, searching for areas of inward toleration of Jezebel in my own soul. You will find it the same as you read.

In the book of Revelation, Jesus confronts this same influence in the Church at Thyatira: "These are the words of the Son of God, whose eyes are like blazing fire and whose feet are like burnished bronze. I know your deeds, your love and faith, your service, and perseverance, and that you are now doing more than you did at first. Nevertheless, I have this against you: You tolerate that woman Jezebel, who calls herself a prophetess. By her teaching she misleads my servants into sexual immorality and the eating of food sacrificed to idols…I will strike her children dead. Then all the churches will know that I am He who searches hearts and minds…" (Revelation 2:18-21, 23).

God has something against the Church of America. We have tolerated Jezebel. Since we have tolerated her, America's children and the children of our churches are being destroyed. However, a standard is being raised up that will produce prophetic sons and daughters who will carry the moral authority that can turn the nation.

A young friend of mine had a vivid dream of the pop icon, Madonna, surrounded by men. He walked up to her and said, "I'm going to marry you." She replied mockingly, "I would never marry you!" As he walked away, he heard her tell those around her, "I have him wrapped around my finger." She started to seduce him and a powerful spell began to take control of him. Suddenly, my friend came to his senses and cried out, "I know who you are! You're Jezebel!" and the demonic spell was broken.

This dream changed my friend's life forever. He repented from a love for the world and an inward toleration of Jezebel's seductions in his life. He now stands as a holy testimony for God, even as he works in the midst of Hollywood's seductive entertainment culture. The Church in America must come to such an awakening as well.

Thank God for John Paul Jackson and his gift of revelation. May God use this book as a sword to slice through our deception and prepare the way for a great Elijah revolution that can break the curse off of our lives, our families, and our nation!

LOU ENGLE
Pastor, Harvest Rock Church, Pasadena, California
Founder, Elijah Revolution
http://www.elijahrevolution.com

CONTENTS

ACKNOWLEDGMENTS

MANY PEOPLE ARE INVOLVED in the making of a book. First, my dearest expression of appreciation goes to my beloved wife, Diane. She has continually encouraged me and offered valuable insights throughout the fifteen years it has taken to write this book. Many demonic attacks have caused me to shelve this book several times. Yet the Lord kept speaking and saying, "Don't give up on it."

Diane has valiantly weathered each harassing storm the enemy sent our way to abort this book's publication. Her prayers, insights, and keen ability to hear the voice of the Lord have enriched this manuscript, as well as my own life. This book may prove to be the most difficult book that I will ever have to write.

I want to acknowledge the efforts of all who contributed to this book. My heartfelt thanks goes to Marla Wessel who assisted me fifteen years ago in developing the original manuscript. I wish to thank three intercessors who made valuable suggestions to the manuscript: Tina Santizo, Linda Nail, and Jo Beth Kested. I also wish to thank those who lovingly proofread the manuscript: Randa Rottschafer, Jane Mitrani, Diane Schechner, Laura Smith, Fenancia Tillema, Ruth Armstrong, Laurie Thompson, Kyndl Sanchez, Vicki Jackson, and Roxanne Stewart.

I want to acknowledge Carolyn Blunk, who served as the managing editor on this project, and her assistant editor, Brett Yates. Their hours of hard work and dedication have turned my meager attempt into a helpful treatise for the Kingdom of God. I also want to thank Ed Tuttle whose designs frame this book.

My heartfelt appreciation goes to Lou Engle who wrote the foreword and to my dear friends who sent their endorsements to encourage others to read and capture the glorious destiny of a coming prophetic generation.

Finally, I want to express my appreciation to my staff at Streams Ministries International for helping me carry the spiritual weight of this exposé. They, in turn, have had to face their own battles as Satan has sought to stop this book from being printed.

Through God we will do valiantly, for it is
He who shall tread down our enemies—Psalm 60:12.

INTRODUCTION

IN THIS BOOK, I have recounted the stories of many who have battled the Jezebel spirit. I hope the lessons and experiences chronicled in this book will be an encouragement to you. However, in reading this book please do not make the mistake of assuming that women are the only ones influenced by this demonic spirit. While it is true that the only clear examples in Scripture were women, I believe that men such as Absalom, Korah, and Balaam operated under this spirit.

I pray that pastors, in reading this book, will restrain themselves from casting stones at the innocent or anyone who disagrees with them. I also pray that they will not mistakenly perceive those with a growing prophetic gift, who are simply immature in church protocol, as having a Jezebel spirit. Hence, throughout the book I have tried to point out the differences between these two spirits, along with some suggested remedies.

Finally, in reading this book, I trust that you will not come to the conclusion that I am against strong, anointed women in ministry. Nothing could be further from the truth! In fact, I was prompted to accept God's call on my life by a very powerful and anointed woman, the late Ruth Ward Heflin.

In 1981, Ruth had been given a dream while living in Jerusalem. The Lord told Ruth to go to Dallas, Texas. She would be given time on a radio show to discuss how God speaks through dreams and visions. The Lord told her that a young man would be listening to the broadcast who was resisting the call of God on his life. He had given this young man dreams and visions. During the talk show, the young man would call in. She would be used to change the direction of his life and help him fulfill his destiny. I was that young man.

So, please understand that I highly value women fulfilling their call in Christ. In the last days, many godly women will arise with an anointing to predict and demonstrate awesome signs and wonders. While many women will exert a boldness, fierceness, and determination that to some might appear overpowering, their lives will also exude submission to God's appointed authority, as all our lives must.

We are on the threshold of the greatest move of God in the history of the world! God wants to visit us in an unprecedented way. This book was written as a call to a prophetic generation that was foretold in Scripture by the prophet Joel. He described a remarkable generation that would have the spirit of God poured out upon them without measure (Joel 2:28-32). Under the anointing of the Holy Spirit, prophetic utterances would arise from both men and women, young and old.

Historically, wherever prophetic voices are being raised up, the enemy will raise up counterfeit voices that mimic the prophetic anointing. That voice is the Jezebel spirit. In this book, I will focus on how Jezebel, as a celestial power, influences the actions of individuals. Knowingly or unknowingly, these individuals will hinder and oppose the move of God in this age.

It is my prayer that God's divine order will come into prominence and that the Church will be aroused from its complacency and tolerance of this spirit. I also pray that God-breathed prophetic ministry and godly intercessors, bearing the mark of humility, wisdom, and discernment, will arise and help to usher in the glorious Kingdom of our Lord.

CHAPTER 1

AN AGE OF APOSTASY

IT WAS AN AGE of apostasy. A nation whom God had called to be His own turned against Him. They exchanged their worship of God for the idols of a people they had once conquered in His name. The king who ruled Israel was the son of a man who gained his kingship through assassination. His name, Ahab, was to become a synonym for evil.

Behind the corruption of Ahab's throne was a woman—Jezebel. Hoping to expand her power by marrying Ahab, she brought destruction on the Israelites. This destruction came through her fanatical devotion to the false gods—Baal, the male deity of power and sexuality, and Ashtoreth, the female goddess of fertility, love, and war. Baal and Ashtoreth rituals involved depraved and licentious sexual practices and abominations. The worship of these idols appealed to the bestial and material elements in human nature. The Baal idol resembled the male sexual organ while the altar to Ashtoreth resembled the female sexual organ. More than 450 prophets of Baal and 400 prophetesses of Ashtoreth served Jezebel's depraved and carnal desires. Human lives were often sacrificed to appease her pagan deities.

Against this abomination, God raised up the prophet Elijah who challenged Ahab and destroyed the prophets of Baal on Mt. Carmel. As a countermove, Satan raised up his messenger to silence God's prophetic voice. It came through Ahab's wife—Queen Jezebel.

We are living in an age of apostasy. Our society has turned its back on God. Sin has infected the Body of Christ and its leaders. However, in the midst of incredible decadence and depravity of our day, God is raising up a prophetic generation that will carry the spirit of Elijah. They will be anointed to perform miraculous signs and wonders and to accomplish great exploits for the Kingdom of God.

Just as he has done from the beginning, Satan is raising up a fierce opposition to this prophetic generation. The enemy has always sought to silence God's prophetic voices and abort intercessory prayer. Its name is Jezebel—a diabolical spiritual force that seeks to deceive, defile, and destroy God's authorities.

While the term "Jezebel spirit" is used in some charismatic circles, few people truly understand how this demonic force operates. A Jezebel spirit is a celestial power that has worldwide influence. It is not simply a demon that possesses an individual. It is a demonic power in the heavenly realm that transcends specific geographical boundaries and can affect nations. Whatever region this power enters, it cojoins and collaborates with the ruling principality of that territory.

Jezebelic powers operate in conjunction with principalities and powers that torment people (Ephesians 6:12). These demonic powers include spirits of religion, manipulation, control, lust, perversion, and the occult. These spirits often work in concert with a Jezebel spirit to build strongholds in a person's mind.

When a Jezebelic stronghold is established in a person's mind, I define this as "coming under the influence of a Jezebel spirit." At the moment this occurs, the individual's rational, reasoning process begins to deteriorate. His or her thoughts and actions become distorted.

For those familiar with computers, you might say that the computer of that person's mind has received a virus that causes it to respond to data in a non-logical manner. It corrupts, re-routes, and distorts all information received from that point forward. Like a computer virus, a Jezebelic stronghold is programmed to manifest when certain keystrokes—or situations—arise. The virus also influences the activity of others in the afflicted one's network. A Jezebel spirit, like a virus, is designed to shut down the network and kill the host, as well as anyone who does not disconnect from the host.

An anti-virus program alerts the computer to the fact that a virus is operating contrary to the laws of the computer program for which it was designed. The anti-virus program then tells the computer how to recognize the virus and discard it. To operate effectively, a computer may need to be reprogrammed with new data—depending on the degree of damage caused by the virus.

This illustration dramatically parallels what happens in the Kingdom when an alien force—a Jezebel power—is downloaded into a church. Its goal is to disable and destroy individuals, ministries, and the church. This will be the result unless God's remedy—a divine antivirus—is applied. If pastors are unable to prevent or detect this spirit's operation, their spouses, children, and church members may fall prey to this overwhelming spirit.

From time to time, all of us are vulnerable to being influenced by this controlling and manipulative power. We all try to control others to some extent. Opening your soul to operating in a Jezebel spirit is a process that occurs over time, and there are no clear-cut indicators of when a person steps over the line. The longer someone operates in a controlling and manipulative way without repenting from doing so, the stronger this spirit grows. Eventually, it will become a way of life for those overcome by this spirit. The primary method for relating to others and gaining control will now operate through this spirit.

Although the illustrations of Jezebel in Scripture are female-oriented, this demonic power does not simply infect women. Men have operated in this spirit as well. When this occurs, they are left weakened and emasculated by the demonic presence. However, it is difficult for men to operate under the influence of this spirit for very long because it needs an Ahab spirit to keep it alive. Instead, the Jezebel spirit commonly operates through women, who use the allure and seduction of this spirit to accomplish their objectives.

By writing this book, I seek to facilitate healing and unity in the Body of Christ. Therefore, I want to caution anyone when applying the term, "Jezebel spirit." As

Christians, we do not want to hurt people unnecessarily—maligning and falsely accusing them. We can actually take on the characteristics of Jezebel—a murderous spirit—when we hunt people down and falsely accuse them. Above all, we must remember that most of those influenced by this spirit are hurting and wounded individuals. The power of the Holy Spirit is available to heal all who are afflicted by this demonic spirit.

The Lord Jesus longs to set us free from what ensnares us. All of us must look at our own sinful natures, as well as that of others, with compassion and hope. Ministry to people and churches who are oppressed by this spirit is desperately needed. It is the time for pastors to be filled with courageous and God-given grace.

CHAPTER 2
UNHOLY ALLIANCES

NELSON TOOK ANOTHER sip of coffee and continued to watch the attractive young woman. She was tastefully dressed in a dark suit and had the look of optimism—a confident handshake and direct eye contact, while soulfully engaging people in conversation. With her penetrating charisma, the woman was vivacious and enthusiastic. She had the ability to draw people to her. She was fun to be with and seemed to be a devoted student of the Bible.

Nelson's church was beginning to shrink. Individuals that he had earmarked for leadership had left. To fill their void, Nelson needed to find new leaders. Each month his desperation increased, as the money from tithes and offerings continued to shrink.

During their times together, the woman suggested her theories on how to increase church membership. A savvy businesswoman, she created a blueprint to steer the church towards a position of dominance. Over the ensuing months, she became more entrenched in the church and began to lead a women's Bible study group.

At the same time, Nelson was puzzled by the woman's beliefs. She seemed to be in touch with the spirit, however, it seemed to be a "dark spirit." This spirit had told her to do unusual things, some of which had previously resulted in immorality. Despite this, Nelson and his wife loved being around this woman. Seeing her potential, they met with the woman often and attempted to mentor her.

As they placed their hopes in her, young women in the church began to rally around this woman. While her influence grew, Nelson's diminished like a slow leaking tire. Each month, the church continued to shrink in members. Then, Nelson's wife began to suffer various illnesses, and his mind became filled with sexual fantasies. To make matters worse, his once amiable church staff became divisive and their vibrant small-groups program began to dwindle.

One day, Nelson called and asked for help. As I began to seek God, a dream came, allowing me to see through the enemy's smoke screen. I relayed what God had shown me, which he affirmed as accurate. But Nelson and his wife still seemed torn. Stalled by indecision and confusion, they continued to give the woman responsibility, leadership, and authority within the church. They admitted that she might occasionally receive counsel from a "spirit guide." Nonetheless, they loved this woman and wanted to help her. What were they to do?

AN UNHOLY ALLIANCE

What I have just described is called an unholy alliance—a relationship that draws you inevitably to dire results, even though you are aware the person willfully continues to sin. Furthermore, it is evident from Scripture that God does *not* sanction such a person being given a leadership position within the church. Nelson and his wife justified their decision not to remove this woman from leadership "for the sake of the Kingdom." Therefore, the Kingdom was compromised by the unholy arrangement, and their church suffered.

Divided Loyalties

A similar situation happened with Omri, Israel's sixth king. To secure and enlarge his kingdom, Omri forged an unholy alliance through the marriage of his son, Ahab, to a foreign bride, Jezebel. This created a political bond between Israel and Tyre. The marriage was meant to seal a peace treaty between the two nations; however, the alliance proved to be a costly compromise. Ceremonially, it required that Israel follow the religious and political protocols of Ahab's new wife. This meant furthering the immersion of Israel into the worship of foreign gods. Therefore, by his plan to enlarge his kingdom, Omri actually positioned the Israelites in harm's way. His need to build a glorious nation blinded him to the consequences of his lawlessness.

By agreeing to take a foreign queen, Ahab knowingly violated God's command. Apparently, he justified his actions in his own mind, but the Lord condemned Ahab as having sold himself to wickedness (1 Kings 21:25). Since Jezebel was a zealous participant in the depraved worship of Baal, a political alliance would have officially endorsed her immoral and idolatrous religious beliefs and inflicted them upon the Israelites. History tells us that is precisely what happened.

Jezebel brought her vile religious practices to Israel. She mandated that stone idols be set atop the high places and erected in God's holy temple. Even if she did nothing else, this flagrant decree alone caused her to be hated by the prophets of Israel. Thus, Jezebel exchanged the profane for the holy. Scripture also indicates that Jezebel was a harlot and an adulteress as well as a practitioner of witchcraft (2 Kings 9:22).

Jezebel had personality characteristics that engendered manipulation, control, sexual perversion, and idolatry. Some rather startling and relevant conclusions can be made about such a woman. I believe an evil spirit motivated Jezebel's actions and bestowed upon her widespread influence.

The influence of this spirit still exists today. It has never been eradicated from the Church. Instead, it has enjoyed an unholy reign. This spirit seems even more entrenched in the Church as the spirit of prophecy is poured out on all flesh (Joel 2:28).

The name, Jezebel, is Phoenician in origin and means "un-husbanded." Although she was married, her lack of submission and her infidelities proved that true marriage meant nothing to her.

While marriage is a picture of mutual respect and submission, Jezebel submitted to no one. Instead, she required that everyone submit to her. Her marriage was merely a political alliance that enabled her to become not simply the queen, but in essence, the acting king! She held the answers to all of the king's problems.

DEADLY DIVA

Jezebel had learned treachery from her father, Ethbaal, whose name meant "like unto Baal." Ethbaal had become king by plotting murder. Thereby, Jezebel's penchant for murder had generational roots. Eliminating someone's life was merely incidental to achieving an objective.

Jezebel was no ordinary woman. She had a flair for the dramatic. Every action she took, every word she spoke must have been done with great passion and unholy abandonment. She was an intimidating figure, a rose with razor sharp thorns. She was impossible to ignore, because to do so could cost you your life.

The way Jezebel greeted Jehu at the top of the wall was more than a casual hello. She painted her eyes and picked out the most alluring gown she could find. She planned a seductive maneuver to entice Jehu, Israel's tenth king (2 Kings 9:6), and to lure him into forming an alliance with her—perhaps by becoming his wife. If nothing else, she sought to intimidate Jehu.

Ahab, King of Israel from 869-850 BC (1 Kings 16:31) was not the only one to succumb to Jezebel's perversions. Her children yielded to their mother's control. Her son, Ahaziah, was guilty of Ahab's sins (1 Kings 22:51-53). Another son, Joram, was killed by Jehu as punishment for all the things his parents had done to God's prophets (2 Kings 9:24-26). Jezebel's daughter, Athaliah, became queen of Judah and just like her mother, she looked for a husband who was weak so that she could carry out her evil practices (2 Kings 8:25-27). As a result, Athaliah's son, Ahaziah, who was named after her brother and may have been conceived through their incestuous relationship, did evil in the sight of the Lord. Both mother and son, as well as the seventy other sons of Ahab and their families, suffered death at the order of Jehu.

Jezebel was a dominant force in Israel. If Jehu had not ordered her thrown from the wall, Jezebel would have had the kingdom to herself. However, Jehu bravely carried out the task the Lord had given him—to do away with the house of Ahab (2 Kings 9:7). In this hour, God is issuing a call to pastors around the world. Will they respond as Ahab or as Jehu?

PEACE AT ANY COST

A spirit of Ahab symbolizes the abdication of authority, or at the very least, passive authority. It bespeaks of a mind-set that avoids confrontation and denies fault. The spirit of Ahab loves the position it has and fears confrontation. Someone with an Ahab spirit would rather make peace at any cost, even if it leads to making an unholy alliance.

An individual under the influence of an Ahab spirit often makes truces instead of covenants, thus prostituting rather than sanctifying relationships. But how can you have a truce with someone whose goal is to destroy you? It is impossible! Nonetheless, an Ahab spirit will always sacrifice the future good for the sake of peace today.

Working in tandem, the spirits of Ahab and Jezebel will quietly form a codependent relationship. Both will need and feed off the other in order to accomplish each one's goals. A pastor who is influenced by an Ahab spirit will need the help of someone influenced by a Jezebel spirit to maintain position and enlarge or entrench a powerbase.

One pastor friend, Russell, kept attempting to introduce me to a specific woman in his church. While this is not unusual—nor is it wrong in itself—Russell appeared to rely too heavily on this woman's input into every decision he made. I cautioned him about developing a codependent relationship, but it was too late. Six months later, Russell fell into sexual sin with this woman.

PLACATING LEADERS

Like many leaders today, Ahab's reign was characterized by trying to placate and pacify Jezebel's demands. He tolerated Jezebel's abominable decrees and practices.

Many pastors embrace an individual influenced by a Jezebel spirit because the person appears to have leadership skills or spiritual insight that a pastor thinks will help their church grow. Some may even convince themselves that, in time, they will be able to spiritually "mature" the individual. But in the process of helping this individual, many pastors strike a compromise and weaken their authority. Remember, Ahab's placating spirit is exactly what gave rise to Jezebel's lethal powerbase.

On several occasions, I have watched pastors remain indecisive and non-confrontational simply from fear that an individual would split their church. One particular pastor was very aware that his chief intercessor operated with a Jezebel spirit. However, he was afraid to address the situation simply because she was intimidating and had influence over others. He thought if he lost any more church members, he would default on his church loan payment. Unfortunately, this situation characterizes many pastors today. Prayer and encouragement are needed for pastors who are caught in this deadly snare.

AVOIDING CONFRONTATIONS

It takes a courageous pastor to confront the strength and obstinacy of a Jezebel spirit. By their actions, individuals with a Jezebel spirit will reveal a pastor's strengths and weaknesses. Pastors will see things about themselves that they might rather ignore. They may react defensively when their authority is challenged. For instance, to quell a revolt, a pastor may respond by appeasing or promoting this spirit. Or in fear, the pastor may decide to suppress all prophetic gifts in the church. Or, the pastor may selfishly even use this person to promote his or her agenda. Any of these responses will damage the spiritual life of a church.

If such a pastor is not checked by a strong board of elders, he or she will leave their church open to domination and control by this demonic spirit. The church will quickly sink beneath an increasing weight of spiritual oppression, crushing healthy spiritual vitality and vision.

A Jezebel spirit defiles everything it touches. That which is holy becomes vile. People will begin to leave a church, not knowing why, simply feeling compelled to go as if they could feel the impending darkness.

Pastors who overreact and impulsively eliminate intercessory and prophetic groups silence their most reliable sources of discernment and revelation. When this happens, a spiritual vacuum is created. The darkness of confusion will then quickly enter. As in a game of chess, if you leave a space unoccupied, your opponent may soon seize that ground. Such a maneuver may allow the enemy to position his own deadly prophets in key places.

Pastors who retreat from exercising their authority may bring injury upon God's people by inadvertently allowing the increased rule of this spirit in the church. As long as the issue is avoided, the problem will only worsen. When it is finally challenged, a Jezebel spirit that has become entrenched in a church is more difficult to dislodge.

CONSPIRING WITH DARKNESS

If a pastor feigns ignorance of Jezebel's wrongdoing, the pastor may become a kindred spirit. Knowingly or unknowingly, the pastor will align himself or herself with this spirit. Their methods and goals will begin to parallel one another. A pastor will also quickly discover that he or she can accomplish their goals by exploiting his or her spiritual mirror image, becoming a conspirator with darkness.

One of two judgments will come to such pastors, unless they recognize their error and repent. They will either fully embrace a Jezebel spirit and become puppet kings subject to strong delusion, heavy depression, and indecision even in the smallest matters. Or, they and their churches will face spiritual famine. God's manifest presence will be removed from their midst. Only the memory of His presence will remain. Most likely, they will not perceive this as God's judgment.

TOLERATING THE ENEMY

When a pastor has a trusted friend who begins to show traits of the Jezebel spirit, it becomes easy for the pastor to justify the person's rebellion or to simply ignore it. Generally, pastors demonstrate tolerance toward those who are "friends." However, the trust and loyalty given to a friend will create a blind spot. A pastor, therefore, will need to step outside the friendship emotionally, view the situation as a pastoral issue, and correct any rebellion.

Ultimately, if a pastor brings correction, people will feel secure under the pastor's leadership and develop trust in godly authority. However, if a pastor fails to correct rebellion, the people will lose respect for the pastor. Church members will regard the pastor with disdain because of the consequences brought upon their church. Confusion will arise and God's purposes will become obscured by a waffling leadership. Furthermore, a pastor who compromises will attract people who compromise. The pastor's anointing will be reduced to a mere drop of what it was meant to be. In the churches of such pastors, the light will grow dim as the Body begins to lose its spiritual cutting edge.

FRUITS OF TOLERANCE

> But there was no one like Ahab who sold himself to do wickedness in the sight of the Lord, because Jezebel his wife stirred him up—
> 1 KINGS 21:25.

Just as Ahab permitted Jezebel to sacrifice children as a form of worship, so our permissive spirit allows the Jezebel spirit to remain the driving force behind abortion in the United States. Through self-promoting, controlling, and manipulative schemes, this spirit also seeks to abort those who are young or immature in the Lord. Moreover, this spirit welcomes false teachers who are driven by the intellectual power of the soul.

Beloved, the hour has come for a new mandate. It is rising up in the land and gaining momentum. God is empowering His Church with boldness and zeal brought about by true apostolic and prophetic voices. In this hour, God desires the spirit of prophecy, which is the testimony of Jesus, to be vibrant in every church. The prophetic spirit will reveal that which is hidden.

VICTORIOUS BATTLES

> Thus says the Lord God of Israel: 'I have anointed you king over the people of the Lord, over Israel...that I may avenge the blood of My servants the prophets, and the blood of all the servants of the Lord, at the hand of Jezebel'—2 KINGS 9:6-7.

At this point in history, a great battle awaits God's representatives—the shepherds of His Church. Pastors are being summoned by the Lord to take on the spirit of valor and to stand up as true kings. Just as Jehu's commission was to rid God's Kingdom of the defiling and demoralizing influences of Ahab and Jezebel, a call is going forth today to remove those same apostate spirits from the Church.

CHAPTER 3

A CORRUPTING INFLUENCE

IN AN EPISODE OF *Star Trek: Deep Space Nine*, entitled, "Paradise Lost," aliens known as changelings infiltrated key positions in Starfleet. These aliens had assumed human form and had taken the appearance of trusted members of the Federation. Their purpose was to create confusion and fear on the Earth. Just as the changelings sent their agents to sabotage the Federation, Satan sends his own dark forces to disrupt the work of the Church. These demonic agents assume our appearance and speak our language, but their allegiance is to another kingdom. Just as the Federation needed to learn to discern the presence of changelings, so the Body of Christ needs to identify those operating under a spirit of Jezebel.

Scott, who pastored a very large Midwestern church, was puzzled about the multiple defections in his leadership team. He had carefully chosen and trained a remarkable team. He now suspected that another staff member was leaving. Then, the light began to dawn: One of his staff members met with a woman who had once been a member of a witch's coven. She incidentally mentioned that she recognized two women who regularly attended the church as being witches from her former coven. Although it was assumed they were Christians, it was later discovered they were still practicing witchcraft. During the church services, the duo would sit on the front row and quietly chant under their breath. Tragically, these witches were able to derail Scott's strong leadership team by sending demonic curses against them.

TAKE WARNING

The apostle John gave a warning to the Church at Thyatira, a city in Asia Minor, concerning a person who had embraced the Jezebel spirit.

> Nevertheless I have a few things against you, because you allow that woman Jezebel, who calls herself a prophetess, to teach and seduce My servants to commit sexual immorality and eat things sacrificed to idols. And I gave her time to repent of her sexual immorality, and she did not repent. Indeed I will cast her into a sickbed, and those who commit adultery with her into great tribulation, unless they repent of their deeds. I will kill her children with death, and all the churches shall know that I am He who searches the minds and hearts. And I will give to each one of you

> according to your works. Now to you I say, and to the rest in Thyatira, as many as do not have this doctrine, who have not known the depths of Satan, as they say, I will put on you no other burden. But hold fast what you have till I come. And he who overcomes, and keeps My works until the end, to him I will give power over the nations—He shall rule them with a rod of iron; they shall be dashed to pieces like the potter's vessels—as I also have received from My Father; and I will give him the morning star—Revelation 2:20-28.

Imagine how the Church in Thyatira felt when they read "I have this against you...." (Revelation 2:4). God gave them a choice: remove the unrepentant Jezebel or suffer God's judgment. Few, if any, decrees are as dreadful as this one. To fall under God's judgment is a fearful thing. When God resists you, nothing you do will prosper. As you come out from under His protection, you will be powerless before principalities and powers.

Removing an unrepentant person from a church is the same principle in which the produce manager at a grocery store does "freshness checks" throughout the day. He knows that one peach with a rotten spot can spoil the entire barrel because the decaying acid will spread to other peaches. Eventually, the entire barrel will become bad because of one bad peach. Therefore, rotten produce has to be identified and removed in order to save the remaining peaches.

This principle of removing sin from the Body was why the apostle Paul commanded the Church in Corinth to remove the young man who was sexually immoral with his father's wife. One man's sin will infect an entire church much like a little leaven or yeast spreads throughout bread dough (1 Corinthians 5:1-12). This was the situation facing the Church at Thyatira. Jezebel's influence was corrupting the church and defiling many. She and her influence had to be identified and removed in order to prevent the entire church from being defiled and disgraced.

LEADING BONDSERVANTS ASTRAY

Jesus warned the Church at Thyatira about this spirit. The Jezebel spirit seeks to destroy and silence God's prophets because in doing so, the enemy destroys the testimony of Jesus, which *is* the spirit of prophecy (Revelation 19:10). By calling herself a "prophetess," Jezebel from Thyatira was leading God's bondservants astray.

Over the centuries, many of the Lord's bondservants, apostles, and prophets have been attacked by the Jezebel spirit. Those who survive the campaign of this spirit often vacate their church posts and move to other locations. Until a pastor finally uses his or her godly authority to remove this spirit from the congregation, mature prophetic voices will stay away. Meanwhile, the Jezebel spirit will seek to implant its own demonic prophets in a church in order to teach the deep things of Satan.

Whenever a pastor fears an individual or a demonic spirit more than God, the pastor is unwittingly admitting, "This spirit is more powerful than God." More than likely this was how the Church at Thyatira came to accept the woman Jezebel as a prophetess and teacher. Obviously they knew her problems, because Scripture says they tolerated her and knowingly indulged her deviant beliefs and practices. More than likely, they were intimidated by her ruthless control and insubordination. Subsequently, she procured a church leadership position.

To agree with a Jezebel spirit is portrayed in Scripture as committing spiritual fornication with her. By allowing an individual influenced by a Jezebel spirit to remain in leadership, the leaders were causing God to judge not *only* Jezebel but the church as well (Revelation 2:22). However, God told them this could be avoided simply by removing the unrepentant individual.

God's Judgments

> ...and all the churches shall know that I am He who searches the minds and hearts—Revelation 2:23.

What a solemn and challenging responsibility faced the pastor in Thyatira! Not only was the Lord going to let all the churches know the results of what happened, but He was going to let them know the judgment—or the blessing—that would happen in Thyatira, if they did not repent. In doing so, God not only judged their actions but their hidden motives that allowed them to tolerate Jezebel's lawlessness.

A Singular Burden

> ...I will put on you no other burden—Revelation 2:24.

The simple yet overlooked phrase in Revelation 2:24 indicates the singular weight of importance that God gave to removing this spirit. The Church at Thyatira was charged with only one task—to remove Jezebel. Since God referred to the task as a "burden," we can sense the extreme difficulty of removing a prophetess who was in leadership. Undoubtedly, it would involve a devoted effort by all the other church leaders, as well as the entire church body, to overcome this morally compromising influence.

I believe that God chose Thyatira to be an example to us today. From that time on, churches around the world would look to this church to learn how and why they must handle this diabolical spirit.

Overcoming a Jezebel spirit will require more than simply ending the self-proclaimed and self-anointed rule of individuals who advertise their spiritual gifts. It also requires that God's leaders humble themselves and repent from using their God-given authority in an unrighteous way, and more importantly, repent for not using their authority.

A PASTOR WHO CRIED "JEZEBEL"

Michael seemed very self-assured and confident. Nevertheless, beneath his charming exterior, he was full of insecurities. At this his second pastorate, Michael faced complaints from church members that reminded him of his first pastorate. Anticipating another failed situation, he began to respond defensively and harshly to any criticism. He grew suspicious and controlling. Easily provoked, Michael would shift the blame for various problems onto others—often charging innocent people with "having a Jezebel spirit." During his third year, a new couple began attending his church. After several surprising encounters, Michael realized that both the husband and wife operated under a mature Jezebel spirit. There was only one problem:

Michael had used the term "Jezebel" so many times that no one believed him now.

To make matters worse, the leadership began to point a finger at Michael's own issues of control and manipulation. Thrown off balance by their suspicions, Michael felt as though he was the person on trial. Six months later, this couple boldly proclaimed in a Sunday morning service they were "anointed by God" to pastor the church. A week later, Michael was forced to resign and the couple became co-pastors. Within a year, however, the church closed its doors!

UNRIGHTEOUS AUTHORITY

> ...for in whatever you judge another you condemn yourself; for you who judge practice the same thing—ROMANS 2:1.

Michael, in pointing the finger, was condemning himself. His actions only served to empower the Jezebel spirit in his church. If he had not been guilty of the same issues, Michael would have recognized the difference between the innocent and those with a Jezebel spirit, thereby avoiding the painful consequences that ensued.

Pastors and leaders must recognize, and then relinquish, *any* methods of control and manipulation they exercise. They must cease to gossip against fellow pastors and other believers, to talk disrespectfully about other ministries, or to reveal personal tidbits shared in confidence with them. Pastors who have privileged information, are sometimes the worst offenders of gossip. They must refrain from talebearing, before the wineskin tears.

Making private accusations and listening to accusations without a proper witness also needs to cease! Pastors must avoid capitalizing upon and exploiting their church members' spirituality, coercing them to do what they want done. This is called "domination" and is a fleshly counterfeit of what it means to righteously exercise spiritual influence and authority. To overcome a Jezebel spirit requires that leaders address *all* rebellion and usurped authority committed by one church member against another. To do this, pastors must be free of these issues as well.

In order for the flock to understand proper authority, leaders need to teach on biblical authority. Overcoming a Jezebel spirit involves recognizing and restoring whatever relationships were overturned and any God-ordained authority that was stolen by this spirit. In later chapters, I will address this more fully.

THE REWARDS OF RIGHTEOUS AUTHORITY

> ...And I will give to each one of you according to your works—REVELATION 2:23B.

Exercising righteous authority has a reward that corresponds to the very thing we have overcome. The pastor who overcomes a Jezebel spirit that seeks to usurp his or her rule will be given a greater sphere of rule and authority. This was what the apostle John said when he wrote the Lord's admonition to the Church in Thyatira:

> And he who overcomes, and keeps My works until the end, to him I will give power over the nations—He shall rule them with a rod of

> iron; they shall be dashed to pieces like the potter's vessels—as I also have received from My Father; and I will give him the morning star—REVELATION 2:26-28.

Three promises are given to those who overcome a Jezebel spirit. First, they will be given widespread spiritual authority over principalities, powers, and spiritual rulers in high places, now as well as in the age to come. Breaking this spirit's power on Earth—individual by individual—disintegrates the rule of dark powers in the heavenlies.

Second, pastors who overcome a Jezebel spirit will be given authority to rule "with a rod of iron." The only other place "a rod of iron" is mentioned is in Revelation 19:15 when it speaks of Jesus. Ruling with a rod of iron does not mean being tyrannical. Rather, one who so rules will find his or her authority conditioned by great wisdom. Such pastors will uphold the discipline and principles of God's Word. When a pastor is like a rod of iron, he or she cannot be easily bent or manipulated.

Third, pastors who overcome a Jezebel spirit will be given the "morning star" (Revelation 2:26-28; 2 Peter 1:19). The morning star referred to in this passage is divine authority and favor.

Both rewards—the rod of iron and the morning star—differ from other rewards recorded in Revelation. Moreover, they carry *much* greater authority than is evidenced today. Although none of the other churches mentioned in Revelation received these three particular promises, neither did they face the formidable task of confronting and removing a Jezebel spirit.

WATCHMEN AT THE GATE

It is imperative to be discerning about those who bring destruction to the Church. It is, therefore, the role of *humble* intercessors to stand as watchmen at the Church's gate. It is the responsibility of intercessors to sound the alarm when they discern someone who might injure the fold. Consequently, it is vital for every church to have a strong intercessory ministry in order to prevent the spirit of Jezebel from doing its destructive work.

How does a pastor discern who are the true watchmen? On the television episode of Star Trek: Deep Space Nine, the changelings were quickly discerned by a simple blood test. Although they looked human, they were bloodless. Likewise, true watchmen can be discerned by what is inside of them. There are several ways their true spirit becomes evident. One way is through their words. Jesus said:

> ...For out of the abundance of the heart the mouth speaks. A good man out of the good treasure of his heart brings forth good things, and an evil man out of the evil treasure brings forth evil things—MATTHEW 12:34-35.

If Jezebelic tendencies exist in an intercessor's heart, then eventually it will be revealed through that person's speech and/or actions. Such a person will sow lawlessness or divisiveness in a church. However, a true watchman does not use his or her position to challenge and belittle pastoral authorities. Rather, the intercessor humbly lifts them up by praying for them.

Another way a true watchman becomes evident is by the fruit of his or her spirit. Scripture clearly defines what the fruits of the Spirit are:

> But the fruit of the Spirit is love, joy, peace, longsuffering, kindness, goodness, faithfulness, gentleness, self-control. Against such there is no law—Galatians 5:22-23.

We must watch to see and to know those who labor among us. We must know them deeply—what they believe, what they listen to, and what they say when they pray.

> Either make the tree good and its fruit good, or else make the tree bad and its fruit bad; for a tree is known by its fruit—Matthew 12:33.

A true watchman is submissive to authority, whereas someone operating under a Jezebel spirit usurps authority. A true watchman does not seek authority, but he or she prays for those who have authority. In a best-case scenario, a watchman who is submitted to the Holy Spirit has the same attitude as David when he served Saul—one of restraint and respect to God's chosen authority:

> The Lord forbid that I should stretch out my hand against the Lord's anointed—1 Samuel 26:11a.

Finally, the most obvious difference between a true watchman and an individual operating with a Jezebel spirit is the motivation, or driving force, behind his or her actions. A true watchman is motivated by love in everything he or she does. In writing his love treatise, the apostle Paul offered the Corinthian church the following gauge from which to discern true and false workers of the Gospel:

> Love suffers long and is kind; love does not envy; love does not parade itself, is not puffed up; does not behave rudely, does not seek its own, is not provoked, thinks no evil; does not rejoice in iniquity, but rejoices in the truth; bears all things, believes all things, hopes all things, endures all things—1 CORINTHIANS 13:4-7.

OUR CHALLENGE TODAY

How will we respond? Will we recognize and confront this counterfeit and destructive voice? Will we deal with our own issues that may blind us or cause us to overreact?

Pastors must arise and lead like Jesus Christ, the bright Morning Star who outshines all other prophetic witnesses and who destroys the works of the evil one. The pastor and the church that seek to obey God in this matter will be given a greater sphere of authority. Remember:

> Be strong and courageous. Do not be afraid or terrified because the Lord your God goes with you; he will never leave you or forsake you—DEUTERONOMY 31:6.

CHAPTER 4

SPINNING THE WEB OF DECEIT

REBECCA WORE AN EMERALD green dress. Although she was not very attractive, Rebecca carried herself seductively. Something about her auburn hair and the way she dressed gained the immediate attention of those around her. As the congregation began to worship, her voice could be heard singing over the others.

Sadly, Rebecca was unaware of the spirit that was driving her need to be noticed. In her mind, she was simply trying to live a spiritual life. However, Rebecca had never addressed the wound that created her need for public affirmation. In fact, when confronted with this in the past, she denied any problems in this area. Nevertheless, her need for recognition saturated everything she did. Consequently, she had to be removed from a church staff position.

Rebecca believed the pastor withheld the recognition she truly deserved. Therefore, she began to subtly criticize him as not being spiritual. She asked others to pray that God would cause him to listen to her, because she felt that God had given her insight that would change the church. When this tactic failed, Rebecca looked for other avenues of support. She found a sympathetic ear with the associate pastor.

Demurely, Rebecca began to ask the associate pastor questions that possessed a hidden agenda. He was unaware of Rebecca's motives and how she intended to use his words to rally grassroots support for her cause. She was planning to overthrow the senior pastor and replace him with the associate pastor. She believed that his sympathetic ear would ensure her further influence and power.

Rebecca began getting bolder in her claims. She used her former church position and began to twist the associate pastor's words, saying the senior pastor was preaching heresy and that he was theologically unsound. She would take the associate pastor's words out of context and insert them strategically into conversations to make it appear as though the associate pastor agreed with her. However, this tactic unraveled when a counselor approached the pastoral team. Several individuals had confided to the counselor that Rebecca had convinced them the church was becoming cultish. This further fueled their insecurities and fears.

The final straw came when Rebecca, while spreading a lie, was overheard by the associate pastor's wife. Rebecca was saying that the entire leadership team had asked for the senior pastor's resignation. She further claimed the senior pastor had vehemently refused, saying he would never leave the church. Supposedly he was going to publicly apologize to Rebecca for dismissing her. When the associate pastor's wife heard all this, she realized what was going on. She shared what she had overheard with the pastoral team. Slowly, the shroud began to dissipate and each leader realized he or she had been subtly turned against the senior pastor after being approached by this woman. The leadership team apologized to the senior pastor for entertaining Rebecca's gossip and becoming ensnared by her web of lies.

How could a church fall prey to a ploy so grievous to God? How were the pastors and leaders deceived? Amazingly, the problem was no more obvious to the leaders of the Church at Thyatira than to us today. Individuals who are influenced by a Jezebel spirit can greatly complicate and confuse many facets of church life, including doctrines and authority issues.

Churches Targeted by This Spirit

No church is too great, too healthy, or too pure to be exempted from an attack by a Jezebel spirit. In fact, the greater the church, the greater the assurance that those with a Jezebel spirit will seek to gain influence and power—unless the pastor, the leadership team, the intercessors, and prophetically gifted individuals exercise their responsibility and withstand this spiritual attack.

A Jezebel spirit can be found in any church or denomination. It is not confined to one particular church affiliation. Although the religious semantics and levels of impact that a Jezebel spirit may exert will differ from setting to setting, the basic characteristics remain the same.

Not all who succumb to a Jezebel spirit consciously set out to destroy their church or to gain power over their pastors and elders. Many are simply deceived into believing they are more spiritually sensitive than others. They tend to assume they are always correct. Seldom are they aware their actions fall into a Jezebelic category.

Certain signs accompany the work of this spirit. Please keep in mind that a single characteristic does not indicate someone has a "full-blown" Jezebel spirit. It may simply mean that the person is spiritually and emotionally immature. In this and the coming chapters, I will describe characteristics of the Jezebel spirit. (For a more concise list, please see Appendix A.)

Whenever a combination of three or more of the characteristics exist, there is a strong indication that an individual is being influenced by a Jezebel spirit. While one trait may be clearly noticeable, other traits may be unseen. A prolonged manifestation of any of these traits warrants a closer look at the individual and the situation.

The Jezebel spirit works best when coupled with a person who has embraced an Ahab spirit, often found in men. Men can also move in a Jezebel spirit. Some may attempt to join with a work of God at high levels of church government, much like Absalom who appointed himself judge and sat at the city gate meeting anyone who had a grievance. Absalom would hug and kiss people, thereby stealing the hearts of the people (2 Samuel 15:4-6). He convinced these people that his judgment would be fairer than his father, David.

Over the years, I have watched assistant pastors and elders flow in what some have called an "Absalom spirit." But it is also a masculine form of a Jezebel spirit. In their need to gain recognition and prove they are anointed, they openly or covertly subvert God's appointed authority and engage in lawlessness, thinking they must take action for the sake of the church and the advancement of God's Kingdom. But they secretly go about building their own empire, which is designed to dismantle any other authority.

CONQUERING THE PROPHET

Andrea began attending a church that was known throughout the city to be a strong supporter of prophetic gifting. Soon, she began to regularly attend morning prayer meetings. Due to her faithful attendance and presumable prayer life, people began to look to her for advice. Andrea became referred to by many as a "prophet." Flattered by the attention, she subtly encouraged that reputation.

Meanwhile, Andrea searched out all who had prophetic authority in the church. She sought out the senior prophetic voice, asking questions designed to flatter him. She also asked him to mentor her. However, behind his back Andrea began to undermine his abilities and gifts. She spread gossip and questioned his prophetic words for the church. By the time he discovered what was going on, the web had been spun. He was perceived as an "old wineskin" that should be discarded and Andrea became the new prophetic authority. Disheartened, he left the church. Within two years, the church lost all prophetic and intercessory small groups, and church membership declined from 800 to 250 people. Saying the church had lost its cutting edge, Andrea moved to another church where she repeated her actions.

As in Andrea's life, the ultimate goal of someone influenced by a Jezebel spirit involves issues of control and in particular, how disagreements with authority figures are handled. Consequently, any prophetic leader carrying a true spiritual authority from God is a threat to someone who operates under this spirit.

Since a Jezebel spirit counterfeits the prophetic anointing in gifts, calling, and authority, a prophetic leader will become a target of a Jezebel spirit, as will a church in which the prophetic is held in high regard. A prophetic church and its leaders must realize that if the spirit of Elijah is going to return, so will its counterspirit—the Jezebel spirit.

In its aim to control the prophetic ministry of a church, this spirit also attempts to pervert potential young prophetic voices. This spirit seeks to lure them onto a supposed spiritual road that is actually a dead-end, so that they never fulfill the call God intends for them.

DIVIDE AND CONQUER

The first move a Jezebel spirit often makes is to gain control by trying to remove the established prophetic authority. If a Jezebel spirit can wedge itself between the people, the pastors, and a prophetic leader, then it will move to overthrow the prophetic leader. Discrediting a prophetic leader through reason, strong opinion, and distorted facts are some tools employed by this demonic spirit. Ironically, the person who operates under a Jezebel spirit will have insights that appear spiritual even to those of the pastoral staff.

CONQUER BY JOINING

To seduce, and thereby, conquer a prophetic leader, someone with a Jezebel spirit will seek to gain favor. This individual will attempt to unite with a prophetic leader in the realm of the spirit, saying "I'm just like you. I seem to know what you're thinking and feeling. We are kindred spirits." However, this soulish tie will attack the prophetic leader's mind, will, and emotions. In some cases, this joining together will display itself with sexual manifestations.

This spirit "talks" spiritually, but its strength is born from the power of the soul, and is ultimately deadly to the gifting of its prey. Some goals of this demonic spirit are to dilute revelation, bring about corruption, defilement, disregard, and disdain of God's true prophetic voice.

A Jezebel spirit seeks intimacy with power. It may use fascination and charm in seemingly innocent ways until it gains friendship and confidence—an illegitimate familiarity the person craves. Just as believers are joined by the Holy Spirit, so an individual with a Jezebel spirit seeks to be joined in soul with others under the guise of the union being a spiritual joining.

Ties That Bind

You can usually track how godly men or women form soul-tying relationships with an individual who operates with a Jezebel spirit. It begins in the realm of the soul. Both men and women will find emotional needs seemingly being met by this person.

For a male leader, this will often translate into sexual needs and desires. The season of seduction may eventually climax in the act of physical adultery. Thus, their ability to keep a covenant is breached. Their influence and authority is forfeited; their ministry is destroyed and God's Kingdom suffers great loss. However, if when being enticed and seduced they discern and resist by the assistance of the Holy Spirit, such destruction can be avoided. Scripture tells us that we are tempted to sin when we are drawn away by our own desires and when we allow ourselves to be enticed (James 1:14). A Jezebel spirit creates desire, longing, lust, and an appetite for sin in the heart of a person. When this urge is not curtailed by the Holy Spirit, it produces an intense craving. Reasoning will *not* change or halt the demands of this spirit. An individual who becomes enmeshed in this seductive spirit must repent and receive deliverance.

For a female leader, this soul tie usually manifests as a consuming and magnetic desire to be around the person influenced by a Jezebel spirit. They will often become best friends or even soul sisters, soul brothers, or soul mates. The person with the Jezebel spirit may attempt to take over the leader's group. As the relationship deepens, the leader may feel as if he or she is being swallowed or suffocated by Jezebel.

Some individuals with a Jezebel spirit form soul ties by praying and by "laying hands on" a prophetic leader, hoping to impart the seed of its spirit. Such people may not know they are imparting a demonic touch. They may also want to pray beside a prophetic leader who is ministering to various individuals. They feel compelled to pray for others, but this urge is not from God.

Another ploy is to flatter a prophetic leader. They may present themselves as a friend with an understanding ear—a kindred spirit—who knows the pain of being misunderstood and rejected. They manufacture warmth, which entices the prophetic leader to become vulnerable and share personal issues. If a prophetic leader has a weakness of rejection, he or she can become blinded to a Jezebel spirit that probes his or her weakness in order to gain authority over him or her. The leader's unmet need to be loved has veiled his or her ability to discern the deception being spun.

A prophetic leader *must* confront this spirit's attempts to flatter and seduce, whether the seduction is physical or emotional. When challenged, this spirit usually cowers at first in momentary humility. However, it will eventually redouble its strength and rise up like a cobra with great verbal assault. Such volcanic rage can become quite formidable.

Once leaders recognize what is happening, many fail to act and remove themselves from the soul tie. Often the soul tie makes them feel guilty for *not* maintaining the relationship. Jezebels manipulatively use this ploy.

Prophetic leaders *must* understand that they have not been given the authority to overthrow a Jezebel spirit. They can only reveal this spirit to their pastors. In Israel, God did *not* ask the prophet Elijah to remove Jezebel. In fact, Elijah exhibited signs of anxiety and depression by sulking and running from her presence. So it fell to Elisha, the next prophetic voice, to forewarn Jehu, to whom God gave the authority to remove her. Likewise in Thyatira, God did not ask the prophets to remove Jezebel. Instead He addressed the pastor, who wields a type of apostolic and kingly authority on the behalf of his flock.

If a prophetic individual tries to deal with another person's Jezebel spirit, it simply counterprophesies his or her downfall (1 Kings 19:2). A Jezebel spirit will often cause prophetic people to run from their responsibility. Prophetic people simply need to remove themselves from relationships with those influenced by the Jezebel spirit and seek their own healing.

SUBDUING PASTORAL LEADERSHIP

> With her enticing speech she caused him to yield, with her flattering lips she seduced him. Immediately he went after her, as an ox goes to slaughter...He did not know it would cost his life—PROVERBS 7:21-23.

The prophetic realm is not the *only* target of a Jezebel spirit. A Jezebel spirit will target a pastor and the church staff, seeking to find the weakest link in order to sever it and gain favor in subtle ways.

For a pastor, it will seem unbelievable that such a "spiritually mature" person could have anything but the highest of motives. The more a pastor is blinded to Jezebel's identity, the more likely he or she will fall prey and embrace the "gifted" person. Over time, it will become more difficult for a pastor to recognize that this individual operates with a controlling spirit that seeks to conquer the pastor and divide the church.

THE ANOINTING ATTRACTS

Troy had a great anointing from God. Thousands attended the churches he had started and to which he had been given oversight. Mighty signs and wonders followed him. He moved in words of knowledge with incredible accuracy. He was disciplined in prayer, fasting, and was an avid student of Scripture. The magnitude of God's anointing on his life was revealed in his sermons and writings. Even in the early days of his ministry, an apostolic mantle was evident. Nevertheless in ignorance, Troy fell into a trap.

While counseling a woman, Troy discovered that she was a witch. Without intercessory assistance, he attempted to deliver her. Pretending to be delivered, the witch built a web of flattery, telling Troy how great he was. She claimed that when he prayed, she felt God's touch like never before.

Shortly thereafter, subtle changes began to affect Troy's life. His hunger for spiritual things began to dissipate. His prayer life, fasting, and Bible study diminished. He excused his disinterest as being due to an ever increasing workload. Thus, the trap was set.

After her departure, two other witches were sent by the coven to attend Troy's church and petition Satan to destroy both Troy and his church. These women attended intercessory meetings and began to exert influence on others as they rose to leadership roles. As their influence blanketed the church with deception, they even convinced the intercessors that Troy's wife was a spiritual hindrance to him. Eventually, they "prophesied" that God would take her life so that Troy would become the great man of God he was destined to become.

One witch became Troy's secretary. Each day, she made constant innuendoes to him and the staff about his wife's shortcomings. Entertaining the lie that his wife was holding him back, Troy slowly agreed with the forces of darkness that "the Lord should take her home." He began to ask God for an illness unto death to come upon his wife. Troy's wife actually became very ill, but when she was near the point of death, God intervened.

Then, Troy's seductive and vivacious secretary reverted to a new strategy. She hinted that his wife had actually been sent by Satan to keep Troy from producing a godly "man-child seed." As unbelieveable as this sounds, she convinced Troy that she alone carried this golden seed that would be birthed from their sexual union. Being enmeshed in such a web of deception allowed these palatable and silly lies to take root in him. Troy eventually divorced his wife and married this woman. Within nine months, he developed prostate cancer and died. The woman inherited all his wealth. She later drew another pastor into her web and married him. He also died.

SLOW AND CERTAIN DESTRUCTION

Troy's story is an example of how someone with a "mature" Jezebel spirit will seek to destroy a man of God through manipulation, deception, and sexuality. This spirit imparts its curse much like the venomous Black Widow spider that destroys its mate after sexual union. Furthermore, with sexual immorality comes a curse of sorcery that results in physical illness and death to the one who joins in this seductive ploy (Revelation 2:22).

Someone with a Jezebel spirit is attracted by the allure of a pastoral anointing. As light draws a moth, so a pastoral anointing draws a Jezebel spirit. Any power outside its own threatens loss of control. This spirit, therefore, drives an individual to do anything to gain and maintain control over others. A Jezebel spirit is ruthless and deceptive, even to the person who manifests this spirit.

When a Jezebel spirit attacks a pastor's wife, the attack may begin to manifest as a barrage of confusing thoughts, as physical or mental illness, or as an emotional breakdown. When a Jezebel spirit becomes more brazen, it will begin to insinuate to others that the pastor's God-ordained destiny is being hindered by his wife's lack of spirituality. As this spirit becomes bolder, the person may begin to pray openly that the pastor's wife change or die, in order for the pastor to fulfill God's call. Obviously, these actions describe the work of someone who has become a "mature" Jezebel spirit.

Not surprisingly, an individual with a Jezebel spirit often tries to become part of the church staff. If a position is unavailable, the individual may try to provoke someone to leave or seek their removal from a position. Even more astoundingly, the individual may brazenly declare to close friends that he or she should have been the pastor, or at least the pastor's wife.

The individual may even suggest she can bear a "godly seed," which could be portrayed as a child or a glorious church. Tragically, when this situation is *not* dealt with, the pastor's marriage often fails and he marries the Jezebel.

As astounding as this may seem, this scenario is played out around the world scores of times each year. Satan is crafty. Whether it's Naboth's vineyard or a new spouse, a Jezebel spirit will stop at nothing until its goal is obtained. The Church at Thyatira was warned about these very issues. We, too, are warned by the Holy Spirit about these issues still present in the Church today.

CHAPTER 5

THE SEDUCTIVE FACE OF JEZEBEL

HERODIAS HATED HIM WITH all her heart. Even though he was now in prison, it seemed his voice would never be silenced. However, this would soon change. Although her lover was an evil man, he would not order the execution of this prisoner who was esteemed as a prophet. He feared an uprising, so she would have to try another ploy.

As much as she hated to admit it, Herodias knew his real lust was for her daughter, Salome. Patiently, she waited to launch her plan on his birthday, which the powerful and the influential would attend from around the empire.

On his birthday, Herod was in great spirits. After the wine had greatly fueled his spirit of lust, Herodias approached her daughter. "Go, Salome, dance for Herod. He'll give you anything you ask for and when he does, ask for the head of John the Baptist."

Dressed in a violet tunic that draped her body, the young girl approached Herod and whispered in his ear. He smiled and then asked her to entertain him. As the beautiful young woman began to dance, her seductive moves enticed everyone in the room, especially Herod. Intoxicated and aroused by passion, he offered to fulfill any wish she might have. As Salome looked secretly to her mother, she smiled and said, "I want the head of John the Baptist on a platter." Bewitched by Herodias' beautiful daughter, Herod was putty in the girl's hands.

THE DANCE OF SEDUCTION

The demonic spirit that inspired Herodias to murder John the Baptist (Matthew 14:6-11) was the Jezebel spirit. The spirit of Elijah that rested on John the Baptist had once again threatened and challenged the spirit of Jezebel. Herod, who had an Ahab spirit, was unable to say no to Herodias' demands. In placating her demands, he got what he wanted—sexual favors. She got what she wanted—the death of the prophet who threatened her rise to even greater power and authority.

FALSE FLATTERY

Flattery is a primary tool used by someone influenced by the Jezebel spirit. Flattery is often used to pry open a door to endorsement by church leadership. Although offering sincere compliments that edify others in the Body of Christ are good, flattery differs in its motive. Flattery seeks to gain approval and recognition from those in authority. Thereby, this spirit only gives in order to get, stealing authority and favor that would rightfully have been given to someone else.

Mistakenly, many pastors believe that a person with a strong prophetic gift automatically possesses the same level of moral character. However, a person operating with a Jezebel spirit—as well as an immature prophetic individual—can portray a very real and sometimes awesome prophetic gift, but remain extremely weak in moral character as well as theology. In someone guided by a sophisticated Jezebel spirit, flattery will transcend and smooth over any differences between people. Flattery may be employed to portray profound admiration. It may seem to endorse the church's vision and direction. Such individuals will speak the same language as the pastor and leaders, but their motives will be to gain position and control. Stripped down, this strategy is "to conquer by joining" in spirit.

Laying a Trap

When flattery is being bestowed by individuals with a Jezebel spirit, they may tell the pastor about the great things the pastor will accomplish, building up false hopes and false expectations about his or her future. Once this trap is set, the pastor will be told at precisely timed moments of weakness that there exists a danger to God's plans; someone or something is holding the pastor back. It may be the pastor's spouse, an elder or even another church member. This Jezebel may be heard praying for God to remove a "mystery" person so the pastor "can become all he or she is called to become." The praying one then guards the identity of the "mystery" person until confident of having a strong base of church support. Then, the identity of the person who is supposedly a threat will be revealed. This usually results in the mystery person's removal from a position of influence. These destructive maneuvers can bring incredible pressures on a pastor, who is provoked to arise and prove his or her worth and anointing to the church.

PITTING ONE AGAINST THE OTHER

Flattery can also become a catalyst for causing division. Usually this ploy is accomplished through creating destructive "relational triangles." In a triangle, Jezebel will befriend person A and person B. However, Jezebel will slowly convince person A that person B does not like him or her. She will also convince person B that person A does not like him or her. Then, Jezebel will appear as a peacemaker who has a deep desire to see each one succeed. By pitting each one's gifting or wisdom against another's, this individual produces jealousy, strife, and contention—even in the strongest of relationships.

There is no satisfying the endless demands of a Jezebel spirit, because there is always something or someone standing in the way of their quest for power. This drives a pastor to discouragement, defeat, and despair. Over the years, I have watched many pastors retreat to another church rather than fight this battle.

Someone with a Jezebel spirit will seek to gain sympathy from many people, especially when confronted. Such individuals will claim they have been spiritually abused. They may use "buzz words" to disarm arguments against them. If a pastor responds defensively to their discourse, he will only reinforce their accusations of being spiritually abused. If a pastor does not have a strong relationship with church leadership, he or she may become trapped in an illogical, unreasonable, or senseless catch-22 situation. The following story illustrates this:

Kevin, who pastored a small congregation of nearly 100 members, began to notice that his worship leader, a man in his late twenties, was taking a lot of liberty during worship. He would often force people to combine various gestures with their praise and worship—dancing or marching around the auditorium. Kevin became troubled because he felt that such expressions should come as a result of the direction of the Holy Spirit, *not* in an attempt to coerce the Holy Spirit to come.

Kevin also observed obvious signs of control and manipulation from the worship leader toward various members of the congregation. On Sunday, the worship leader had publicly challenged Kevin's authority and leadership ability. To complicate the matter, the small church was growing and the worship leader was the only person in the church who could lead praise and worship. Freely, Kevin admitted he couldn't "carry a tune in a bucket."

What was Kevin to do? The worship leader's lawlessness had escalated. Would Kevin have the courage to remove him regardless of the consequences? To do so, Kevin would have to believe in the sovereignty of God. No matter what it would look like initially, the church would become healthier with the worship leader's removal. Thereby, the church would grow correctly.

STRATEGIC AFFILIATION

An individual with a Jezebel spirit strategically affiliates with others in the Body who move in spiritual realms. Such individuals realize that those who are spiritual are looked upon favorably. Therefore, an individual with a Jezebel spirit shares that favor through strategic affiliation. Thus, this individual mounts his or her campaign to win popular and pastoral endorsement in his or her bid for growing influence.

An example of strategic affiliation is seen when the apostles Paul and Silas were on their way to prayer and a woman with a Jezebel spirit joined them. Simply by walking beside them, she insinuated that she too was going to prayer, hoping to win the acceptance of Paul and Silas and those who watched. She also began to proclaim they were servants of God (Acts 16:16). Pretending to be an intercessor, she attempted to gain a spiritual foothold in the city. Discerning her motives, Paul ended up delivering the woman of a spirit of divination. By use of strategic affiliation, this demonic spirit sought to acquire a deeper foothold of influence in the region.

DISMANTLING A WALL OF PRAYER

Robert was the pastor of a growing charismatic church. A woman who had a strong "prophetic" anointing began attending his church. Within a few months, she rose to leadership over several churchwide prayer groups. Unfortunately, the woman began using these groups as a forum to promote her own agenda. Subtly, she began to inject critical venom about Robert. When he discovered what she was saying, he confronted her. But by then, she had widespread support, having spent hours on the telephone with many church members.

The woman blackmailed Robert with a threat of tearing apart the church unless he acquiesced to her demands. Claiming he was a poor leader, the woman said she was forced "by the Lord" to take the actions she did. In their meeting, Robert became unusually confused and actually ended up agreeing with the woman. Eight years later when a similar situation occurred, Robert recognized what had happened to him. But by then, it was too late. His church, which had been declining, was now only a handful of people.

Since the tactic of dismantling a wall of prayer is so successful, someone with a Jezebel spirit tends to infiltrate intercessory groups. This person will try to control the content and direction of prayer. It is only a matter of time before this person become the group's leader. Jezebel spirits usually cause such events by pre-meditated efforts; sometimes the individual is unaware of how their power works. Whether it happens knowingly or unknowingly, however, the driving force is a demonic spirit.

As the individual devises a takeover, it is not unusual for the current prayer leader to experience sudden or prolonged health problems or mental confusion. Eventually, the current leader will resign. The individual with a Jezebel spirit begins to counterfeit true prayer leadership. This takeover will be accomplished in such a manner that seems natural. Eventually, false humility and mock timidity will disappear. The individual will begin to declare rather brazenly that he or she knows the mind of God and how everyone should pray.

When this happens, the energy given to prayer will seem to increase. Unsuspecting and undiscerning individuals will be tempted to think things are getting better. However, this energy will begin to dissipate. Remember, energy derived from soulish passion will always be short-lived. Only that which is born of the Spirit of God will be maintained by God's Spirit and bear fruit that remains.

If left unchecked, this takeover will bring an inevitable end to the intercessory group. One-by-one, individuals will be drained of the desire and the grace to pray. The group will begin to dwindle. Thus, the watchmen in God's house will be scattered and the church will be left unprotected. A demonic coup will have taken place. Too few in leadership will notice the spiritual chill that now blows through the church, though all are affected by it.

FALSE DREAMS AND VISIONS

> When he speaks kindly, do not believe him, for there are seven abominations in his heart—PROVERBS 26:25.

Tactics intended to frustrate the Kingdom of God will come easily to those operating with a Jezebel spirit. They seek recognition by trying to manipulate situations to their advantage. From deep within their soul, they will conjure up an unusual number of dreams and visions. They may also "borrow" dreams and revelations that God has given to others, presenting them as though God had given them the revelation. Or, they may enhance and embellish their own dreams to make them seem even more spectacular and impressive. Scripture offers an excellent perspective of God's view on this matter.

> Therefore behold, I am against the prophets who steal My words every one from his neighbor...Behold, I am against the prophets

> who prophesy false dreams...and cause My people to err by their lies and by their recklessness—Jeremiah 23:30-32.

Carrying False Burdens

These individuals will carry false burdens from the Lord, hoping to appear spiritual. They may even believe they are speaking God's words, unable to recognize the deception under which they are operating. Once such a person gains an open door to the pastor, it is not uncommon for Jezebel to flood him or her with "revelation" that has supposedly been received from the Lord. Every situation will be subtly manipulated to cast a favorable light on the individual operating with a Jezebel spirit, thus bringing attention to the schemer rather than to the Lord. As this spirit's roots take deeper hold in the person's soul, righteous and redemptive fruit eventually become non-existent.

Creating Spiritual Dependency in Others

The first Sunday she visited, Brian noticed her. He watched her carefree way of meeting people. Secretly, Brian hoped she would demonstrate the leadership qualities he desperately needed due to recent church growth. Brian and his wife, Linda, invited the woman to supper to learn more about her. That evening, Brian did not discover as much as he had hoped, yet the woman seemed confident and able to hear from God. She shared how God had led her to his church. Brian hoped this was a sign of the Holy Spirit's impending move, the very thing for which he had been praying.

In the church services, the woman began giving prophetic words with seeming humility. Her speech was gentle and gracious, mixed with tears. It made her "prophecies" seem from God. But as she became increasingly vocal, giving words Sunday after Sunday, Brian grew uneasy. He also became uncomfortable that the woman was attracting members who were needy, insecure, and spiritually naive. When the woman's husband finally came to church, Brian felt somewhat relieved. Her husband always seemed to be away on business trips.

Everything seemed to go smoothly until four months later. Brian began to notice that several leaders uncharacteristically had missed meetings and church services. Not long after that, Brian heard rumors that this couple had started a church. Making matters worse, the woman had telephoned church members and urged them to leave Brian's church. Brian was hurt and upset, but what could he do? Should he address it publicly? Should he go to the couple privately, following the procedure outlined in Matthew 18?

APPEARING MORE SPIRITUAL

When an individual with a Jezebel spirit is put in a leadership position, he or she will try to create an impression of walking on a higher spiritual plane than most. Others may feel less spiritual or intimidated, when they are around this person. This ploy creates an emotional dependency in others. Feeling spiritually inferior, they will seek out the Jezebelite for spiritual guidance. Furthermore, if any question the Jezebelite's spirituality, they may experience harassment.

New believers are especially prone to this kind of subtle, but nonetheless effective, intimidation. Some may choose to pull away from the person, but those who choose to stay will usually comply with the Jezebelite's demands rather than face being ostracized. Once joined to this spirit, believers who are weak or easily intimidated will find it difficult to remove themselves from the grip of the Jezebelite.

FALSE HUMILITY

> The integrity of the upright will guide them, but the perversity of the unfaithful will destroy them—PROVERBS 11:3.

Once people with a Jezebel spirit receive recognition, they respond initially with false humility. This ploy will serve to further entrap you and convince you of their spirituality. However, this misleading meekness will be short-lived. False humility is actually a mask for deeply rooted pride and presumption.

Once this false humility is discarded, this kind of person will proudly offer many "prophetic" promises. The Jezebelite will foretell of a great kingdom coming to the pastor. However, when these soulish predictions fail to materialize, a pastor's faith is deflated as hope deferred makes the heart sick (Proverbs 13:12). A dark cloud of depression may engulf the pastor, who begins to fight the urge to detach from his or her congregation.

By this time, the Jezebelite will have become entrenched in the church. Evicting this person or curtailing his or her usurped authority, would seem to bring about an exodus from the church, although it would save the church. If the pastor knew what to do, he or she no longer can summon the strength to fight back. If the pastor were to address the situation, he or she thinks that would risk making his or her leadership look foolish simply because the pastor was the one who placed the Jezebelite in the leadership position.

EMOTIONAL BLACKMAIL

In leaving—or in threatening to leave—the Jezebelite usually discredits the pastor and claims the pastor is not as spiritual as people had thought. The Jezebelite may also maintain, "I'm *just* concerned for the people."

At this point, emotional blackmail ensues. Since a Jezebel spirit now holds the key to the emotional balance of the church, the individual will be able to confidently hold the pastor hostage. The pastor then becomes captive to obey directions from a demonic spirit. When this happens, a pastor may sense a sudden "call by God" to leave and shepherd another congregation in another city.

However, this situation will most likely recur until this pastor recognizes and admits to having an Ahab spirit and tolerating a Jezebel spirit. A similar fate awaits him or her at the new church. As long as these areas remain unhealed in the pastor's life, Satan will continue to exploit him or her by bringing another Jezebelite. God's severe mercy allows this tormentor to continually plague a pastor until he or she acknowledges, repents of, and finds healing from operating with an Ahab spirit.

CHAPTER 6

DEADLY PLOYS

IN THE STAR TREK episode, "A Taste of Armageddon," an alien leader, Anan 7, took Captain Kirk prisoner. The alien contacted the spaceship, U.S.S. Enterprise, in a voice sounding like Kirk's and ordered the ship's shields lowered and everyone on board beamed down to the planet. Upon their arrival, the alien intended to kill them all. Scotty was in command of the ship. When he heard the order, he sensed that something was wrong. Scotty asked the computer to analyze the voice. It affirmed that the voice came from a voice duplicator and *not* from Captain Kirk.

Like Anan 7, a Jezebel spirit may speak in a prophetic voice that sounds familiar, but it turns out to be counterfeit. Just as Scotty knew his captain's voice, so believers need to discern the voice of their Commander, the Lord of Hosts, from that of the enemy.

It is difficult to pinpoint how the powers of darkness deceive and counterfeit God's voice or presence.

Demonic spirits may sound spiritual. They may even use Scripture to achieve their goals. A discerning ear, however, will detect both accuracy and motive.

In the beginning, these people may start out by saying right things in wrong ways. They may believe that God has specifically chosen them, when in fact, their grandiose ideas may stem from voids in their life. In time, they will begin to believe their relationship with God is more spiritual than the relationship others have with the Lord.

The apostle Paul gave this admonition to Timothy:

> Be diligent to present yourself approved to God, a worker who does not need to be ashamed, *rightly dividing the Word of Truth.* But shun profane and idle babblings, for they will increase to more ungodliness. And their message will spread like cancer. Hymenaeus and Philetus are of this sort, who have strayed concerning the truth, saying the resurrection is already past; and they overthrow the faith of some—2 TIMOTHY 2:15-18.

In this passage, Timothy is warned to "shun profane and idle babblings" because they will spread like cancer. Although Paul is speaking of people spreading heresy, the same principle can be applied to those operating under a Jezebel spirit. Like those who promote heresy, individuals who operate with a Jezebel spirit sow falsehood, division, strife, and discord in "the name of the Lord."

In order to combat this corruption and divisiveness, we must become like Timothy, rightly dividing the Word of

Truth. The Greek word used for "divide" in this passage is *orthotomeo,* which means literally to "dissect correctly." Therefore, with the gift of discernment, we can correctly dissect the hidden motives of someone operating under a Jezebel spirit.

DEFENSIVE POSTURING

When confronted with the matters described above, an individual with a Jezebel spirit will usually respond with statements like, "I'm just trying to help" or "God told me to do this." Their response comes from an imagined sense of God's will. Offering such a response becomes a trump card because saying that God is the commissioner of the action should end all debate. However, this dead-end logic must *not* be allowed. The battle lies not in the realm of reason of fighting logic with logic. It rests in the realm of the Spirit that divides between soul and spirit.

Tragically, many pastors have found themselves lacking the sharpness to overcome the persuasive arguments of a Jezebelite. Many pastors are too distracted with the activities demanded by their congregations. Often a pastor has too little time to spend in the Word and in prayer.

Pastors are on-call 24-hours a day, seven days a week. As a pastor, I have experienced and witnessed the enormous demands and pressures placed on these overseers. Eddie and Alice Smith accurately describe this in their book, *Intercessors and Pastors: The Emerging Partnership of Watchmen and Gatekeepers.* Due to family and time constraints, many pastors are unable to discern someone's correct application of Scripture or the spirit of error inspiring its misuse or distortion.

UNREASONABLE AND UNYIELDING

Seeing themselves as spiritually superior, a Jezebelite often believes God has provided a hedge of protection around him or her, isolating them from any deceptive spirits. Some even believe they are immune to sin and deception because of their "spiritual maturity." Believing they have been highly favored and chosen for some spiritual high place or position, such individuals conclude they have a divine, secret strength. Thus, their emotional support comes from within their subjective experience, rather than from God and His written Word.

Eventually, such individuals become unteachable and unyielding. Over time, they will become deceived to think they are infallible. They become unable to listen to others, because others "have not had a direct revelation from God" like they have. Therefore, to reason with them or to question them—so they believe—demonstrates the height of sin and carnality. Such individuals usually demand blind obedience.

As I teach on this subject, I am always amazed by the number of individuals who share experiences of following someone with a Jezebel spirit. They describe how the leader mystically reveals God's supposed plan of action for them. They are then told what to do, when to fast, when to abstain from sexual intimacy with their spouse, and so on. Some are even coerced by the Jezebelite into praying long hours and giving large sums of money.

APPEALING TO OTHERS

> There is a way that seems right to a man, but its end is the way of death—PROVERBS 14:12.

Seeming to have great spiritual insights into church issues, individuals operating with a Jezebel spirit usually do not share these insights *first* with the pastor, according to Biblical pattern. Instead, they share their insights with others, building a powerbase of support. Clearly, this is a departure from Scripture. In God's Word, a prophet always went directly to the king—not to the people—following the proper protocol of leadership and God opened the door of access to that realm.

It is actually a spirit of rebellion that drives these people to take their insights about the church directly to others. Perhaps their revelation comes from a genuine word of knowledge or a word of wisdom. But when individuals overstep their boundaries, their revelations have become mixed with their soul and becomes corrupted.

Pastors need to notice the little foxes that destroy the church vine (Song of Solomon 2:15). Such caretaking does take time, which few pastors have. However, until lawlessness is addressed, that leaven will continue to permeate until the whole lump—or church—is leavened.

Individuals who give way to a Jezebel spirit do not perceive the value of praying revelation versus speaking it. Deceived by ulterior motives, these individuals appeal directly to others. In doing so, their realm of influence is broadened and the spiritual mysteries they espouse are admired. Thereby, such individuals come to expect honor and adulation from others.

> How can you believe, who receive honor from one another, and do not seek the honor that comes from the only God—John 5:44.

Alleging mystical insights, an individual with a Jezebel spirit will rarely find things going well in a church. Wanting others to become dependent upon his or her input, the person must prove spiritual maturity that even surpasses that of the pastor. Thereby, the Jezebelite's followers will keep their eyes upon their new spiritual leader. Consequently, the Jezebelite will demand to have the "last word" in many church matters.

Individuals operating with a Jezebel spirit will generally be tuned to the latest books, tapes, or messages by various national, spiritual leaders. However, Jezebelites will distort and take out of context certain elements within messages in order to endorse their own teaching. Thus, the original words or teachings are misused and laid open to criticism because of how they are erroneously retold.

Brian pastored a large church which also had one of the strongest Christian schools in the state. One of his intercessory prayer leaders had begun to tell several mothers in the school that they were married to the wrong man. She said that for these women's well being and that of their children, they needed to divorce their husbands. If they would do this, within one year their "God-appointed" soul mates would appear. Several marriages were thus impacted because they already had existing problems in the marriages. The intercessory leader who had gained a "following" had convinced everyone that she was hearing from God.

Often individuals with a Jezebel spirit eagerly seek to minister prophetically to people, driven by a need for affirmation. They seek out people to proclaim revelation, hoping to gain favor and a devoted following. Mature prophetic voices, on the other hand, seldom seek out people because it drains them immensely. Only when God directs him or her will a mature prophetic individual step forward and minister.

Unfortunately, many who follow a Jezebelite are often new Christians or those naive about spiritual gifts. The naiveté of these new believers is badly exploited. They often become filled with delusions of grandeur that will only occur if they submit and follow Jezebel. Over time, spiritual strain is often heavily placed on young or immature believers. However once they express loyalty, a Jezebelite will do "an about face."

Much like Dr. Jekyll and Mr. Hyde, a Jezebelite may tell some about their remarkable spiritual gifts that the Jezebelite alone can develop. Then, as they express their spiritual insights, the Jezebelite scolds them for supposed errors or immaturities because the Jezebelite must always maintain the upper hand. Spiritual confusion ensues and replaces healthy spiritual development. This ploy is designed to keep followers dependent on Jezebel, trapped in low self-esteem, and addicted to Jezebel's teaching and charms.

> Many will follow their destructive ways, because of whom the way of truth will be blasphemed. By covetousness they will exploit you with deceptive words; for a long time their judgment has not been idle—2 PETER 2:2-3.

This ploy produces a toxic cycle that continually eats away at a person's self worth, leaving naive young believers doubting that God speaks to anyone, including pastors and prophets. Consequently, the true prophetic office that God desires to restore is made suspect to those tainted early in their spiritual walk by the influence of a Jezebel spirit. Whether in the home or in the church, a Jezebel spirit always damages trust in God's true authority.

PRIVATE PRAYER SESSIONS

When it comes to praying for individuals, Jezebel prefers private places. In this way, hurtful innuendoes, implications, and left-handed compliments that are spoken cannot be heard by others or directly challenged. If confronted, these Jezebelites will usually deny having said anything, or insist they were misunderstood. Consequently, it is hard to catch Jezebelites undermining pastors, prophetic leaders, or churches.

It is also quite common for someone with a Jezebel spirit to show up at someone's house without notice, saying the Lord told him or her to go pray for a particular need. This need will often be somewhat elusive and nebulous. There have been times when a Jezebelite will "invent" a future event that must be stopped. Later, when the invented calamity doesn't manifest, the Jezebelite will claim the prayers were answered.

Without witnesses, a pastor will have little success trying to verify the specifics mentioned in these private settings. Thereby, the Jezebelite manages to elude the evidence that a pastor needs to confront the issue. To establish the Jezebelite's guilt, a pastor will need two or more witnesses. Usually, if the pastor prayerfully waits and keeps track of specific issues, witnesses will come forward and God will build the pastor's case. Until then, a spirit of confusion acts as a smoke screen and clouds any confrontations made by a pastor. The Jezebelite will leave the confrontation unscathed, while the pastor is left embarrassed, shaking his or her head.

Seeking Others to Teach

"This is the proverbial straw that breaks the camel's back!" thought Steven who had put up with the woman's constant demands to teach questionable material. He could not prove it was scripturally wrong, and based on her righteous appearance and demeanor, Steven had allowed the woman to form a home group for prophetic people.

But now she had crossed the line, mixing in Greek mythology and New Age teaching. She claimed that an angel of God had given her "the golden hammer of Thor" to hammer out and forge issues of the Kingdom. Steven wondered how an angel could have given that to her? Why did he let her continue teaching in church circles? Why didn't he stop her two years ago, when she first approached him about teaching others? Now she had her fingers in everything. Pulling her out of leadership roles would be like trying to pry an octopus' tentacles off its prey. There just were not enough hands to go around.

Beneath the woman's soft and gentle demeanor was a mixed-up person whom, unfortunately, many considered to be the most spiritual person in the church. A few elders even considered her more pastoral in gifting than the pastor. Furthermore, she was spreading a lie that Steven was only serving as pastor for the money. She claimed that God would remove anyone—including the pastor—who dared come against her. Recently, she had approached Steven privately and demanded his resignation! How could Steven detach the tentacles of this spirit, at this late date, without killing his church?

TWISTING SCRIPTURE AND REWORKING DOCTRINES

> ...there will be false teachers among you, who will secretly bring in destructive heresies—2 PETER 2:1.

> ...by her teaching she misleads my servants—REVELATION 2:20.

A person operating in a Jezebel spirit will seek to teach church doctrine in order to gain a controlling grip on the Body. However, their doctrines will be incomplete, inaccurate, and full of holes. Scripture will usually be taken out of context and misapplied. Even if the person's teaching begins correctly, in time it will deteriorate because it has no deep root. Gradually, a transition will occur. Progressively, the Bible will be ignored, and mystical ways will take a more prominent role.

Often this person's disciples become confused. Those who are naive will profess allegiance. They will dismiss any questions or concerns initially, thinking they just don't know enough Scripture. Others will wonder: This person seems godly, how could his or her teaching *not* be from God?

Directly or indirectly, a Jezebel spirit will subtly spread doubts about the pastor, church leaders, and other prophetic individuals, especially those who do not endorse the Jezebelite.

Reckless Words

> Behold, I am against those who prophesy false dreams, says the Lord, and tell them, and cause My people to err by their lies and by their recklessness. Yet I did not send them or command them; therefore they shall not profit this people at all—Jeremiah 23:32.

Those with a Jezebel spirit will seek to gain credibility by speaking prophetic utterances. However, these prophecies are the product of their own imaginations. As God's spirit begins to lift off them and their reputation fades, they will take information they know and mix it into soulish prophesies, telling people what they want to hear. The result will be a strange mixture of half-truths with a powerful allure. For example, obtaining a piece of information from outside sources, the Jezebelite will announce it to the pastor as if it were a prophetic word. When it comes to pass, the Jezebelite will appear to be a true prophet. This practice is very manipulative and deceptive. God hates it!

Likewise, individuals with a Jezebel spirit will prey on a pastor's poor memory. Because the pastor does not clearly remember word-for-word what was said, Jezebelites will twist or give "new" meanings to their previous prophecies. Thus, they will ensure that all of their prophesies are perceived as totally accurate. They are not looking for accountability, or receptive to it. Consequently, they will tend to be evasive and abrasive to truth, and dislike any demands for accuracy and accountability. Rarely will they admit an error. However, they may concede, only to survive and fight another day.

On the other hand, men and women with a prophetic calling will welcome accountability and demonstrate mutual submission as they grow in godliness. They will concede to making mistakes because they understand that a prophetic gift matures with time.

FALSE PROPHECY

Giving a false prophecy does not simply mean speaking an untrue word. It may mean that a false, lying, and unclean spirit is speaking through a person who is giving a prophetic word.

Instead of Holy Spirit-given revelation, the Jezebel spirit uses a spirit of divination, which in the Greek is literally called *python*. Much like the woman in Acts 16:16, Jezebel's theology may contain accurate insight, but an unclean spirit operates through the person.

Usually, it takes great discernment to discover which spirit is speaking—the Holy Spirit or the unholy spirit. An immature or unsuspecting hearer may not be able to discern the difference. A mature prophet can discern a Jezebel spirit, thus "separating the holy from the profane" (1 Corinthians 14:29; Ezekiel 44:23). Remember, the hallmark of the Holy Spirit is always purity, truth, and sincere love.

EAGERNESS TO IMPART

> For I long to see you, that I may impart to you some spiritual gift, so that you may be established—ROMANS 1:11.

Counterfeiting the doctrine of the laying-on-of-hands (Hebrews 6:1-2), a Jezebel spirit likes to impart its anointing through the laying-on-of-hands. However, the Jezebelite's touch carries a curse. Ask yourself: If it is *not* the touch of God, what spirit is touching you? When a Jezebel spirit is imparted, a dark spirit is deposited into its victims. Obviously, an individual with a Jezebel spirit is *not* someone that you want to have ministering to people in a prayer line! Even if such people are unaware of the Jezebel spirit operating through them, they are still capable of passing on this demonic spirit to others.

Such impartation may result in what appears as a healing, as demons of affliction are shifted from organ to organ. Or, the Jezebelite may want to pass on a "higher" level of spiritual anointing. They may claim their higher anointing can break through walls or chains that have held back an individual or a pastor. They usually claim that God has told them to do this.

Such individuals are always presumptuous if they think they have this level of authority. In essence, they are declaring to be greater than their pastor. Imagine trying to impart something you have to your pastor in order to increase his greatness! Such thinking is twisted. According to Scripture, it is *always* the greater who blesses the lesser (Hebrews 7:7).

An individual's motive distinguishes godly prayer from soulish, manipulative, and carnal prayer. The hidden motive behind such prayer is to increase recognition and elevation for the Jezebelite. Praying for your pastor is necessary and should be practiced on a regular basis. In fact, forming a prayer shield around a pastor is essential to win today's Kingdom battles. Once again, I recommend the book, *Intercessors and Pastors: The Emerging Partnership of*

Watchmen and Gatekeepers that offers suggestions for appropriate boundaries between intercessors and pastors.

APPEARING RELIGIOUS

> Take heed that you do not do your charitable deeds before men, to be seen by them—MATTHEW 6:1A.

Individuals with a Jezebel spirit will almost always exhibit a religious spirit. They may appear to be the most spiritual individuals that you have ever known. They may portray having deep and intimate relationships with the Holy Spirit. However, a closer inspection will reveal that their actions are based on what they think you need to see, to convince you of their spirituality. Perhaps such people will be the first to cry, wail, or mourn, claiming a burden from God. But this behavior will simply be a ruse, meant to promote them in the eyes of others. Often, they will let others know the many hours spent in prayer or in fasting or the faith they have in giving all their money away. The "righteous" deeds of Jezebelites are *always* done for everyone to see. These actions only serve to promote and to enlarge the kingdom of self.

Believing they are "special instruments" of God, such individuals often isolate themselves from others and take separate paths, feeding their independent spirit. A religious spirit blinds them to the sober knowledge of the deception they have bought into.

Like a tidal wave, deception floods the mind, deepened by the continual need for sensual—even sexual—stimulation. Some will begin to view communion with God as a sensual thing. In ignorance, they may begin to commune with evil spirits, and eventually claim that God has entered their body as in a sexual union. They will privately tell others they have actually become the "bride" of Christ. They will even begin to experience physical sensations of a sexual nature, thinking they are giving themselves to the Holy Spirit, just as Mary did. Among women, that is actually the work of an incubus spirit. In men, a succubous demon seduces them.

Experiences Are Dramatized

It is common for people with a Jezebel spirit to entertain a strange mixture of Christianity, New Age, and eastern religions. Their religious actions are meant to convey many mystical experiences and impress others sufficiently so that they will be accepted in the way they deeply desire. A Jezebelite's actions normally will be overly exaggerated. Their vocabulary and orations will become unnecessarily dramatized. As this spirit matures its grip on a person, his or her voice may change when giving a prophetic word. Sometimes an unnatural voice will be manifested, as though the vocal inflection would prove that God was with them. This is no different than channeling. A spirit—not the Holy Spirit—is using the individual's vocal chords.

Although every man or woman of God has a sense of destiny and purpose, this divine purpose should *not* be confused with a Jezebel spirit's false spirituality. God's purposes in our lives lead to humility, but Satan's purposes in our lives cultivate self-promotion. The intent of the heart is always the dividing line between the two.

FAMILY LIFE IN DISORDER

Scripture says that before we can be in any type of leadership, our family must be in order, our children in good standing, and our mate in one accord with us (1 Timothy 3:1-4). How can you manifest a prophetic spirit to restore families (Malachi 4:6), if your own family is destroyed or in disarray? You cannot impart what you do not have! Furthermore, you have no authority to impart that which you have not been able to build in your own life.

Instability often exists in the family life of someone plagued by a Jezebel spirit. This spirit will breed negative attitudes, behavior, and individuals. Families can be destroyed by this spirit.

Individuals who operate in this spirit can be single or married. If a Jezebelite is married, that one's mate will be spiritually weak, miserable, or unsaved. They often become lazy, sluggish, and repressed.

If the spouse is male, he will allow his wife to dominate and control him, but secretly he despises and hates her for it. As she becomes more aggressive, he becomes more reclusive. Sexual intimacy between them takes a back seat to her spiritual needs. He quietly begins to search for other means of meeting his needs.

Because of his anger, he may turn to flirtatious acts, pornography, cybersex, voyeurism, or other ways to alleviate his relational pain and make himself feel good and in control. A Jezebelite will often maintain control over her husband through the marriage bed. She rewards his obedience with sexual gratification. If her husband rebels, she withholds sexual intimacy.

Often, the husband of a woman who operates with a Jezebel spirit is not able to stand as the priest of his household because a Jezebel spirit destroys the family priesthood, just as Jezebel destroyed Jehovah's priesthood and emasculated King Ahab. If he is a believer, this spirit will cause him to forsake his priestly, God-given responsibilities as the spiritual leader of his home.

In some cases, the husband may offer some spiritual nourishment. He may even lead family devotions. Such actions are allowed by the Jezebelite to make her look good, so that others—or even himself or herself—are unable to recognize her veiled control. In reality, she continues to hold the real authority in their home. Aware of the biblical teaching on divine order in marriage, she may decide not to demonstrate her power openly when friends visit. However, she will instantly reinstate her power and position when she is alone with her husband.

In some cases, both husbands and wives will operate in a Jezebel spirit. When this happens, it becomes formidable as their demonic spirits work in unison. However, much like a Queen Bee, the woman will continue to retain the upper hand. The husband, even if he appears to be strong, will be her slave. His duty in looking strong is to make her look even better.

Looking to Other Men

A woman who operates with a Jezebel spirit may claim that she wants her husband to assume the spiritual leadership of their family and that if he did, she would submit to him. But, if the earlier scripting has been etched on the husband's soul, nothing will change.

Her husband's weaknesses may cause the Jezebelite to be drawn to and spend time with other men who demonstrate spiritual headship, thus attempting to fill the void in her marriage.

Eventually, her husband will become so demoralized that he will cease going to church, preferring to stay home watching television or engaging in other substitutes for his wife's affection. Especially he may retreat into his vocation, where he can feel manly, in control, and powerful. He ceases to listen with respect to his pastor—after all, how can he listen to a pastor who can't see through his wife's spiritual facade?

She may coerce the pastor to intervene and act as the head of their household. However, if she is not submissive to her husband, she will not be submissive to the pastor, any other leader—or to God. It's just a matter of time before the pastor also feels the sting of her emasculating jabs.

CASTRATING HER HUSBAND

A Jezebel spirit will influence a woman to criticize and belittle her husband, telling him he's not spiritual enough, bold enough, making enough money, or that he's holding her back from the ministry God has awaiting her. She may apply subtle, manipulative pressure on him by simply sighing and commenting how nice it would be to have this or that, knowing they can't afford it. She may also imply that if he really loved her, he would work harder to provide for all her needs and desires.

Such manipulative ploys put incredible pressure on a man and increase his resentment. It may also cause him to flee into the arms of another woman who is more sensitive to his needs and who makes him feel appreciated and successful as a husband.

In God's order, the authority over the wife is the husband, the authority over the husband is Christ, and the authority over Christ is God the Father (1 Corinthians 11:3). A person with a Jezebel spirit may talk about submission and obedience to her husband, but both her husband and children know that it's all talk. It is *not* reality.

Children who grow up in a family environment in which a parent operates with a Jezebel spirit will be profoundly affected as adults, in ways many do not realize. While I am not a psychologist or an expert on childhood issues, I have noticed through hundreds of encounters, interviews, and testimonies that the following results are most often encountered.

IMPLICATIONS FOR DAUGHTERS

Daughters reared by a domineering mother may manifest masculine or overtly aggressive behavior. Becoming like their mother, they may repress their true femininity, regarding it as a detriment. Seeds of rebellion, manipulation, and control have been sowed into their hearts by a domineering mother and in turn, they may begin to operate with a Jezebel spirit.

Blind to the true source of their pain, some will embrace the women's rights movement or a goddess movement like Wicca. Sadly, even if a young woman longs for a man to fill the void left by her father, she may find it difficult to trust men, as well as God the Father.

IMPLICATIONS FOR SONS

Whenever parents are not fulfilling their rightful roles in marriage, their sons will become confused about their masculinity or become sexually aggressive and seek to subdue women by force. Young men may also respond to their mother's browbeating by becoming overbearing tyrants, and thereby seek to dominate their wives and children. Male subjugation of women is often motivated by resentments against a domineering mother figure.

Some young men may express their resentments toward women and overreact by running from them. Or, they may respond to their unfulfilled needs for a father's affection and authority by being attracted to the same sex, if a particular man eroticizes the masculine void in his life.

When Warren was 18 years old, he had prophetic gifts that were being touted as extraordinary by nationally known leaders. Even as a young man, Warren had been taken to the Third Heaven. He could tell you with amazing accuracy when you would be visited by an angel or give you a date something would happen and it would come to pass. However, Warren had a secret obsession. Although many women found him attractive, Warren was deeply attracted to men.This attraction began when Warren was 9 years old.

His mother pastored a pentecostal church. His father, who was cold and distant, took little interest in the church, the family, or in Warren. When an evangelist came to town to hold his yearly meetings in their church, Warren noticed his mother's attraction to this man. The evangelist, who recognized Warren's prophetic abilities even at this young age, approached Warren's mother about the possibilities of the young boy's traveling with him during the summer months. He said that he wanted to train Warren. She was thrilled. During this time, however, Warren was sexually molested by this man.

When Warren told his mother, she refused to believe him. Warren always suspected that his mother's inability to believe him stemmed from his belief that his mother was having an affair with this evangelist. A strong and domineering woman, she dismissed Warren's pain and accused her son of lying. Tragically, Warren never recovered from this incident or his mother's anger toward him.

Since Warren's father was emotionally distant and unavailable, the visiting evangelist began to fill the masculine role model in Warren's life. Although Warren fought his homosexual tendencies, he was always looking for a man to replace his father. His anger toward his mother further fueled his attraction to men.

As Warren's prophetic gift was recognized, he would have periodic sexual liaisons followed by long periods of anguished repentance and abstinence. Each time, the Lord would return the anointing to Warren. Then while ministering in a foreign country, Warren became ill and was unable to recover. He was sent home and was later diagnosed with AIDS. Warren died at age 32.

CHAPTER 7

UNCOVERING THE ROOTS

KORAH AND HIS FOLLOWERS had been planning to launch a revolt for quite some time. It was evident that Moses and Aaron were old and feeble. Their leadership had only brought further wandering in the desert! Korah and his fellow Levites had continued to challenge Moses and his ridiculous demands. Looking across the great congregation, Korah felt confident that Israel would be stronger under his leadership. Someone like himself must arise and oppose the old man.

Suddenly, Korah heard a voice cry out. It was the voice of Moses. "Depart from the tents of these wicked men!" Moses proclaimed to those near Korah. "Touch nothing of theirs or you will be consumed by their sin!"

As people began backing away, Korah and his family—as well as his followers and their families—stood at the door of their tent. What was Moses up to now?

Facing the congregation, Moses began to announce, "By this you shall know that God has sent me to do these works, for I have not done them of my own will! If these men die naturally like everyone else, then the Lord has not sent me. But if the Lord causes the earth to open its mouth and swallow them up with all that belongs to them and they go down alive into the pit, then you will understand that these men have rejected the Lord" (Numbers 16:28-30).

As soon as Moses finished speaking, Korah felt the ground tremble. Suddenly, the earth split apart beneath his feet. Korah, his family, and all their belongings fell into the abyss. Then the ground closed over them. Although it all happened in a matter of seconds, Korah must have felt the horror of knowing he was about to die and that he had come under God's judgment. Those around them fled, trampling over one another, fearing that God's judgment would touch them, too. Then without warning, a strange fire came out of Heaven and consumed the 250 followers of Korah.

1. A Root of Rebellion

Korah had exalted his will above that of Moses. Likewise, a Jezebelite will believe his or her assessment of a pastor's leadership is correct and attempt to launch a revolt. Since God places all authority in position, rebellion against that authority is lawlessness against God. (I will say more on the spirit of lawlessness in Chapter 9.)

For those who operate with a Jezebel spirit, rebellion is at the core of their being. Thinking they have heard from God, they exalt their will above God's will or above pastoral authority that God has placed over them (Hebrews 13). Whenever our will is served by our desires, we are worshipping our self-interests, not God's. We, in essence, have become our own idol.

God equates rebellion with witchcraft, which is defined as power gained by the assistance of evil spirits (1 Samuel 15:23). It makes little difference whether an individual is cognizant of the evil spirits influencing him or her. In Scripture, Jezebel was distinguished by witchcraft (2 Kings 9:22a). So, it should not be surprising that a Jezebel spirit operates through witchcraft (rebellion), even in the early stages of this spirit's rule in someone's life.

Imposing on Others

The spirit of witchcraft imposes its will by manipulating others. Raping the value of each individual, witchcraft bypasses an individual's decision-making capabilities and establishes its own "higher" authority at the expense of its victim. It may involve an expression of illegitimate authority that has been usurped. It may also involve an unrighteous expression of legitimate authority. For instance, a pastor may use his or her authority unrighteously by manipulating others in the Body.

At the heart of such actions is an attitude of irreverence—devaluing an individual who is made in God's image. This spirit also portrays disrespect for the preciousness of the human will. God gave us the gift of free will and God Himself does not violate it.

Manipulating others does not make an individual a witch—someone who has covenanted with Satan. Nor does it mean the individual is a practitioner of magic, hexes, potions, and incantations. But it suggests that a person is masking his or her true intention.

A Jezebelite allows others to become sacrificial pawns in order to accomplish his or her plan. Its followers are simply convinced the Jezebelite is right and the pastor is wrong. Initially, most believe that by imposing their will they are only seeking to build God's Kingdom. They are not in touch with their own rebellion that blinds them to what God is doing. Those who practice manipulation in their homes and in personal relationships will do the same in church settings, unless the error is corrected. For a church to flourish, however, control and manipulation must cease.

THINGS DONE IN SECRET

In Scripture, the word most often used for witchcraft is the Hebrew word *anan,* which means to cover or to act covertly. This is exactly what the Jezebel spirit does. Although an individual may not be a practicing witch, nor a mature Jezebelite with the aim of destroying a church or pastor, he or she may still have a spirit of witchcraft.

A person can be a Christian and operate in the spirit of witchcraft without realizing it. This spirit has long been hibernating in the Body of Christ. Sadly, it operates through some of the Lord's chosen vessels. Even mature prophetic or intercessory individuals can periodically operate under the influence of this spirit, if there are doors that remain open through old wounds. Evidences of these wounds not being healed would include struggling with feeling overlooked, undervalued, or rejected. Or struggling with bitterness, criticalness, and anger.

For example, Terry and Lisa were active in church for their entire fourteen years of marriage. Terry had a great job in telecommunications and Lisa loved staying at home with their children. Terry was a good man. He just wasn't passionate about spiritual growth. Playing golf on Sunday was more relaxing than attending church.

Lisa had sought to obey God, but it always seemed to result in misunderstandings, dashed hopes, and eventual pain. It seemed that every church they attended had major problems. They always seemed to find themselves right in the middle of the fray.

Sobbing at the kitchen table, Lisa could not understand why they had been asked to leave the church. They were only trying to help people. After all, she could not help it if she "sees" what others do not. The pastor could be a great man, but he would not listen to her. If only he would. Many stood beside her. Why didn't the pastor? The person overseeing the prophetic ministry was totally against her. Still, Lisa had managed to become the assistant prayer leader and had overseen seven of the fourteen prayer groups. She dreamed one day of leading them all.

Since childhood, Lisa had always wanted to be a pastor. If given the right situation, she would lead the church through intercession. She would make their prayer ministry the largest in the state. She would be key to the pastor's success. With her strategic know-how and his authority, they could have built the largest church in the city. Missionaries would have been sent to the nations and hundreds of prophets would have been trained with the new training program that she longed to implement. It was a shame that someone's petty jealousy had stopped her.

As Lisa listened to herself, she noticed anger and bitterness spewing out of her mouth. "Why not?" she argued with herself. She had been wronged again. She knew Terry would simply shrug his shoulders and give her a token response, "I'm sorry." Lately, she had wondered if their marriage would make it. Sometimes she wondered if she had married the wrong man.

Lisa does not know it, but she had already embraced the first level of pride and self-promotion that would lead her down the road to greater deception by a Jezebel spirit. One of the initial evidences of a Jezebel spirit influencing a person is how the person handles disagreements with authority figures. It is not wrong to disagree with a leader; it is what you do with the disagreement that may be Jezebelically inspired. We must follow the proper protocol for conflict resolution as outlined in Matthew 18. We also need to consider the examples of Esther and Haman, David and Saul.

SELF-CENTERED BEHAVIOR

Like Lisa, a believer influenced by a Jezebel spirit may not intend to destroy a church. However, individuals who operate in varying levels of rebellion and witchcraft have destroyed many churches. Thus, witchcraft is able to work through an individual who tries to take control.

Manipulative control is strengthened with each successful endeavor. Full of self-pity and pride, an individual's soul is endangered by deeper demonization. This type of witchcraft can be performed without occult involvement, even by Christians who profess Jesus as their Lord. People who operate in more mature forms of witchcraft are determined to impose their will, no matter what the moral cost. In the case of Jezebel, her use of manipulative control resorted to murder.

Not only is witchcraft displeasing to God, it hinders relationships in which honesty is vital. Since witchcraft violates the will of others and their ability to choose, it greatly damages a husband-wife relationship. It is also destructive in parent-child relationships and relationships with other family members. In situations in which conflict arises, those who operate in this spirit refuse to communicate truthfully, and sometimes not at all. Furthermore, they will employ artful, unfair, or insidious means to gain advantage and achieve their goals, thinking their cause justifies their actions.

Today, God is crying out for godliness and righteousness to arise. When God appoints leaders, it is a prophetic statement that He intends to advance His Kingdom on Earth. Therefore, every advance comes through God's appointed leaders. A Jezebel spirit will seek to abort God's advance by usurping the rule of pastors and leaders.

The summons to take dominion and authority in the Earth is *not* a call for oppressive domination. Domination is actually a fleshly substitute for the godly exercise of true, God-ordained authority.

2. A ROOT OF BITTERNESS

> ...looking carefully lest anyone fall short of the grace of God; lest any root of bitterness springing up cause trouble, and by this many become defiled—HEBREWS 12:15.

Rebellion, in all its forms, has several roots, one of which is bitterness. Bitterness opens a door by which a Jezebel spirit slithers into a person's soul undetected. Bitterness often takes hold in our lives when we feel we are being overlooked for recognition or honor. Self-pity sets in and people, knowingly or unknowingly, begin to seek ways of getting attention to display the gift they believe they have.

Bitterness resides in our soul, because it is a mental stronghold linked to selfishness and pride. Bitterness may be directed toward God or anyone whom God endows with authority. Since bitterness often is a reaction to a perceived injustice or to unjust authority, it will provoke a person to react against all authority, whether just or unjust.

Bitterness brings despair. But since bitterness is tied to pride, this despair will drive people to design schemes that promote their gifts. Bitterness is truly sinful. It deeply damages people and leads to lawlessness. As with all sin, bitterness must be recognized, repented of, and healed through God's grace.

SOUR FRUIT

A root of bitterness will produce varied fruit. It may birth immorality (Hebrews 12:14-16), lifelong anger and resentment, or a pattern of broken relationships. Moreover, a root of bitterness is contagious. A bitter spirit will infect the spirit of many others.

The Cross is the stopping point for all bitter roots. Jesus alone is the Great Physician who can deliver us from demonic torment. His anointing alone turns us from our rebellious ways. A bitter, rebellious heart can be transformed into a grateful, obedient heart, as it is touched by the grace of God. After such deliverance, the person must decide to submit to God-given authority. Submission is a decision—rather than a feeling—which an individual makes. A continual practice of submission will produce meekness. Remember, Jesus said that the meek will inherit the Earth (Matthew 5:5).

3. A ROOT OF BONDAGE

> For you did not receive the spirit of bondage again to fear—ROMANS 8:15A.

A root of bondage leads to fear and produces spirits of legalism, depression, servitude, enslavement, and control. Someone enslaved to a Jezebel spirit—either as its vessel or as its victim—cannot taste true liberty.

Scripture says that wherever the Spirit of the Lord is, there is freedom (2 Corinthians 3:17). Freedom brings about responsibility and accountability. Yet, those who operate with a Jezebel spirit will welcome responsibility, but not accountability. They will perceive accountability as slavery and avoid it like the plague.

Often individuals in the grip of this spirit are unable to sense their adoption as a son or a daughter of God. They feel isolated and uncared for. While striving to meet their own needs, they embrace a victim mentality because life "owes" them something. Even if they are given an extravagant gift, they exude a lack of gratitude, feeling they deserve whatever was given to them. In fact, they always feel more should have been given to them.

4. A ROOT OF FEAR

> For the thing I greatly feared has come upon me, and what I dreaded has happened to me—JOB 3:25.

Fear, which is a lack of faith, opens the door for a Jezebel spirit to enter an individual's life. A mindset of fear may begin in childhood. It then continues until an individual's soul gains rule and begins to control him or her. A spirit of fear—a mental stronghold of the soul—may lie to a young girl. It will whisper, "I will protect you. I will be your refuge from other people's domination. I will give you control." This spirit's deception happens subconsciously because it bypasses cognitive understanding and moves directly to influence an individual's actions. Therefore, a spirit of fear causes you to learn to react to situations with fear.

A spirit of fear *always* gains its influence during our weakest moments. These moments usually follow on the heels of an episode in our life that has left deep scars on our psyche. Weaknesses can also arise from spoken fears of our parents and others. Unfortunately, many well-meaning parents use fear to control a child, rather than developing a child's ability to make wise choices.

A root of fear can be removed by the Spirit of God. But individuals must be willing to pay the price of prayer, patience, and forbearance. They must also desire to forgive any authority figure who has wounded or abused them.

MENTAL STRONGHOLDS

Lies spoken by seducing spirits are *very* subtle. They arrive as thoughts "spoken into a soul" by a cunning and shrewd evil spirit. At first, the thoughts seem logical and just. Once they are embraced, believed, and accepted, these thoughts become deeply embedded into our subconscious mind. They become a way of thinking, or in other words, a mental stronghold. Your conscious mind may never knowingly process the thoughts that enter it from that point on, unless you receive revelation from God and discern that a demonic spirit is trying to control your thoughts.

Most strongholds take root during our childhood years. Generally speaking, your parents probably did not have the discernment to nullify such attacks of spiritual warfare. Even those parents who were able to discern a lying spirit often were not adequately versed in the Word of God to teach their children how to defend themselves against such attacks. Consequently, we have all become potential prey for Satan's lying snares (2 Timothy 2:25-26).

To agree with a lying spirit is to become its prisoner. Such dishonest spirits are demanding prison guards. The same spirit that works *through* and *for* them also works *against* them, to keep a person from escaping. In a twisted way, these demonic prison guards will try to convince an individual that their prison cell is actually a vehicle that will bring about their long-awaited position of honor. But it is an illusion.

Whenever we accept the enemy's lies, we then willingly accept rejection, insignificance, and insecurity. We begin to doubt having a loving heavenly Father. Consequently, a stronghold of fear will produce untold anxiety and depression (Proverbs 12:25).

Once Christians are able to recognize these strongholds, they can find true freedom. Removing a spirit of fear will sever a major root of the Jezebel spirit. Freedom and inner healing for past wounds are accomplished by renouncing false trust in an evil source and by receiving renewed trust in the Lord Jesus. More will be said about this in Chapter 12.

5. A Root of Pride

> Mystery, Babylon the great, the mother of harlots and of the abominations of the earth—REVELATION 17:5.

> ...for she says in her heart, 'I sit as queen, and am no widow, and will not see sorrow'—REVELATION 18:7.

Pride is the tap root of a Jezebel spirit. Pride involves lifting or elevating yourself in order to rule in stature or influence. A spirit of pride is contrary to the Holy Spirit.

Mary, the mother of Jesus, is a good example of the antithesis of pride. When the angel Gabriel announced that she would bear the Savior of the world, she pondered over the mystery of why the Lord chose a humble maiden for such an awesome destiny (Luke 1:46-55).

The spirit of pride is also unlike the heart of Esther, who humbly entreated her authority to hear her petition. Because of her meekness, her cries were heard and a nation was saved.

Nor is this spirit of pride typical of Deborah's heart. As a prophetess and a judge of Israel (Judges 4:4-9), Deborah did not want to presume or wrongfully take leadership that belonged to another. Instead, she stepped into leadership *only* at the insistence and invitation of the leader.

ACTIVE WAITING

Anna had just finished lighting the last candle in the temple. The autumn chill had come earlier this year. But on this morning, the cool air seemed particularly refreshing and her prayers seemed alive and unhindered. Perhaps it was the fast she had just ended. But soon, Anna knew she would see the Light of Israel and of the world.

Years ago the Lord told her in a vision that if she would pray for the coming of the Messiah, she would live to see His arrival. Since her husband had died, Anna had set her heart to serve the Lord daily—from morning until evening—for the past fifty-seven years. At times, it had been hard to persevere, but the Lord had helped her. People kindly brought her provisions. How could she not serve Jehovah Jireh? He truly provides!

Across the courtyard, she saw Simeon coming to say his prayers. Today, he also arrived earlier than usual. She watched as he knelt and raised his hands toward Heaven. The intense presence of the Holy Spirit was in the Temple. Walking around the porch area near the altar, Anna fell to her knees sobbing great tears. God's presence was so powerful. When she arose and walked toward the courtyard to pray for others who would come that morning, she gasped as she passed one of the huge pillars that held up the temple's roof.

Simeon was speaking with a rugged looking young man and his beautiful young wife—both were radiant. As Simeon took their little baby in his arms, tears flowed down his face and beard. When he lifted up the child to bless him, Anna knew in her spirit that Simeon was holding the Redemption of Israel. As Simeon began to prophesy over the child, Anna was led by the Holy Spirit to go throughout the temple proclaiming God's promise was fulfilled. The Messiah had come!

For nearly sixty years, Anna served in the temple with meekness, contrition, and steadfastness (Luke 2:36-38). Self-promotion was not evident in her life. Others called Anna a prophetess, but she did not. As a result of her humility, God exalted her.

DESPISING MEEKNESS

Jezebelic pride is the antithesis of humility. In Scripture, Jezebel is portrayed as glorifying herself and living luxuriously. Full of presumption, she decided to "sit as queen" (Revelation 18:7). This arrogant spirit will despise the lowly estate of a widow or of any woman. This puffed-up spirit views meekness and humility as inherently worthless and debase. As such, this spirit despises subordination to authority because to be submitted to authority would require a sacrifice too great to offer. Instinctively, this haughty spirit uses seductive qualities to lure others into its schemes. Desperate for attention, people under the dominion of this spirit desire the infatuation and adoration by others, who are then led to their death.

A SEXUAL TEMPTRESS

Several years ago I listened in amazement as David shared what had happened to him. He seemed to have the perfect life: a beautiful wife and a job that he loved. His church was bursting at the seams. David was frequently in the newspapers. Everything seemed to be coming together for David, except in his marriage. It had been months since he and his wife had been sexually intimate. Their marriage was becoming strained. He kept planning to take some time off from work.

Then, David began noticing other women. After seeing them in church, he would fantasize about them. One woman in particular caught his attention. He was pleased to see her name scheduled in his calender one day. Feeling more excited about seeing her than he should have been, he decided to guard his emotions cautiously.

The appointment went smoothly. The woman seemed vivacious and eager to serve. She secretly told David that her attractiveness had been a disadvantage in other churches. Two weeks later, she returned again. This time, she was wearing a full length fur coat which didn't seem strange at the time since it was beginning to turn cold outside. As she entered David's office, he closed the door, as was his usual practice since his secretary's desk was just outside. Standing in the middle of the room, the woman began to tell David how anointed he was.

She shared a vision of him preaching to kings and presidents, and she wanted to help him get there. She revealed that God had given her some insight. Looking into his eyes, she told him that she was aware he and his wife had not been intimate in a while. She knew his loneliness. Appealing to his pride, she said that David and other great men of this age were like "King David." Her role was to help the king in any way she could. Just as it was for David and Solomon, one woman could not satisfy the sexual needs of a man with such a great calling.

Intoxicated by her tantalizing words and sensuality, David stopped breathing for several seconds. Then in a bold move, the woman dropped her fur coat revealing her nakedness. His heart pounding with anticipation, a powerful seduction came over him. Moving around the side of his desk, David touched her and gave into the craving that had gone unmet for so long. During the sleepless nights that followed, waves of shame and guilt washed over him. He wanted to run, to turn back the clock and erase what had happened. Eventually, David resigned from the ministry. His 3,000-seat building was later sold at an auction.

> I find more bitter than death, the woman whose heart is snares and nets, whose hands are fetters. He who pleases God shall escape from her, but the sinner shall be trapped by her—ECCLESIASTES 7:26.

The pride of our anointing can be the seed to our eventual downfall. It can lead to a fatal attraction.

THE COMING DECEPTION

Nearly 2,500 years ago, the prophet Zechariah described a spirit of pride that would hide behind a coming deception involving women. I believe he was shown a vision of the Jezebel spirit arising in the Earth today (Zechariah 5:5-11). Zechariah saw a basket that was divided into six parts. The number six is the number of man, depicting fleshly effort. When the basket cover was raised, Zechariah saw a woman sitting inside. When the woman tried to escape, an angel forced her back into the basket and placed a lead weight over the cover. Then, two women with wings like a stork took the basket to the land of Shinar or Babylon, where this woman would sit on a lofty pedestal. The Lord called this woman, who was a demanding and prideful spirit, "Wickedness."

Today, women who strive for power, position, and rule often unsuspectingly embrace an Antichrist spirit. This spirit will urge, push, and cajole women to demand position and authority, much the way the women's rights movement has operated in our day. Thus, these women fall into the snare of fulfilling Zechariah's prophesy.

A spirit of pride makes it very difficult for an individual so captured to repent. The person will need to realize that humility before God is priceless. He or she will need to give up a defensive posture against authority and usurping another's authority—particularly male authority. If such individuals repent of a spirit of pride, they will be delivered from that great and hideous deception.

Rooted in Our Spirits

> Beloved, let us cleanse ourselves from all filthiness of the flesh and spirit, perfecting holiness in the fear of God—2 Corinthians 7:1b.

We are told to cleanse ourselves at the root—which resides in our soul—as well as in our spirit (2 Corinthians 7:1). To ignore our soul or flesh will only perpetuate its fruit. Our spirit will become contaminated if our soul rules over it.

In announcing the Lamb of God who takes away the sin of the world, John the Baptist said, "...the axe is laid to the root of the trees..." (Luke 3:9). In a similar way, we must kill more than just our superficial natures if we are to bear godly fruit. We must examine and deal with the motives of our hearts and sever the deep roots in our soul, particularly if we are to be involved in individual, corporate, and national repentance.

Facing Yourself Honestly

When a Jezebel spirit becomes entwined with a human soul, the roots of the demonic spirit must be discerned. This understanding comes from the Holy Spirit who awakens our spirit to His lack of rule in our lives. He does this by conviction, not condemnation.

God must reveal the point of weakness at which a demonic spirit has access into a person's life. In closing this door, a person will eliminate the threat of that demonic spirit's returning. Any lingering threats that may try to reopen this door must also be dealt with. Therefore, a continuing spiritual vigil must be maintained until complete healing has taken place (2 Corinthians 13:5).

Under great stress, people who have seemingly been freed from a Jezebel spirit may fall back temporarily into former patterns of manipulation and control. Although they may have repented and been delivered of this spirit, their weak or wounded areas may not have had sufficient time to heal. Old habits may resurface. For this reason, if leadership does not pay attention, such individuals may again become a problem.

OUT OF CONTROL BEHAVIOR

If an individual's problems began as a result of a dominant father or mother, an individual may need to question themself with whom he or she vies for control. The person may still be in bondage to a controlling mother and may have married a strong mate with whom he or she competes for control. If the threat of losing control is merely perceived, such a person may have a general fear of authority or may overreact by challenging any authority figure for control. Sound spiritual reasoning *must* be made in order for the individual to trust that others will not dominate, bruise, or belittle them in the future.

Such individuals will readily sense an accusing, critical, or judgmental attitude towards them. This will quickly shut the door to any ministry of restoration. To minister deliverance will require great compassion. Remember, ministry succeeds when God initiates it and when His skill and wisdom are present.

Change Is a Process

Once an individual is freed from this demonic spirit, his or her spirit must be healed and strengthened. The entire process will take time. The person must be given time to mature spiritually. To be placed on leadership would be premature and should *not* happen until deliverance, healing, and restoration is completed. A new foundation will need to be laid in the person's life. This may be difficult for a pastor to do. Especially if the pastor is timid, fearful, or angry at what the individual has done.

It is not unusual for the person who has operated with a Jezebel spirit to have a true prophetic call from God. This gift has simply been perverted, distorted, and misused. Redemption, healing, and maturity can be wonderful gifts that destroy the work of the evil one. Perhaps this is why Satan desires to pervert the prophetic gift—so it will not damage his own empire.

Pastors should take caution. They should not try to heal this wound lightly. Handling the situation poorly—by granting mercy when a firm stand should be taken, or by overreacting to the person—may cause the wound to deepen and result in irreversible damage to the individual. If the person's gift is reactivated too quickly, it will bury the person under the weight of adulation.

No matter what spirit oppresses, they *must* refuse to defend themselves and justify their behavior. They must search their heart and repent, turning away from sin. They must confess their sins to the Lord, who promises to forgive and purify (1 John 1:9). Repentance is vital to the restoration process (2 Corinthians 7:10). Until full repentance comes, God cannot truly bless and heal them (Isaiah 59:20).

In trying to help, leaders need to demonstrate mercy to the wounded individual. Remember, it is God's kindness that leads to repentance (Romans 2:4). Encourage them so they are not hardened by sin's deceitfulness (Hebrews 3:12-13). Avoid doing things that would cause them to refuse healing (Matthew 18:7). Be careful to not demonstrate an arrogant or hostile posture toward them. Any attempt to control them may drive them further into rebellion.

A FORERUNNER PROPHETIC SPIRIT

Centuries ago God sent His messenger, the prophet Elijah to confront Jezebel and her false prophets who were leading God's people astray. In these last days, God is releasing a prophetic message across the Earth. He is raising up men, women, and children who will be empowered and anointed with the spirit of Elijah. They will confront the spirit of Jezebel (Malachi 4:5-6).

As a forerunner spirit, the spirit of Elijah will once again "make ready a people prepared for the Lord" (Luke 1:17b). As we make ready for His coming, we need to lay the axe at the root of our fleshly natures (Matthew 3:10) and bear fruit worthy of the Lord.

CHAPTER 8

THE POINT OF NO RETURN

KENNETH, WHO PASTORED A large church of several thousand members, was experiencing an unusual number of problems. Indecision plagued his leadership, unity among church members had begun to unravel, and the church had come under extreme financial hardship. A spirit of sickness and infirmity had begun to powerfully assault the intercessors and their families. It was the first time that such an unrelenting attack had come against the church. Even Kenneth's wife had become very ill.

In the midst of these calamities, a "savior" appeared—a woman stepped forward to run the daily prayer meetings. At first, Kenneth viewed the woman as an answer from God, despite the fact that two intercessory leaders warned him about this woman. These intercessors claimed to have been given dreams and words of knowledge about this woman, which were hard for Kenneth to believe.

Then, a church member led by the Holy Spirit happened to go to the new prayer leader's house. As she approached the door, she was startled by strange noises coming from inside. Concerned, she peeked in the front window. She was horrified to find the woman kneeling on the floor, chanting, and sticking pins in dolls that were dressed like Kenneth's wife and other various church leaders. Later, it was discovered that the woman was praying for the death of Kenneth's wife so that she could become his next wife. Sadly, the woman was deceived into thinking that her actions were for the ultimate good of the church. She truly believed Kenneth's wife was holding the church back.

PROGRESSIVE DEVELOPMENT

Left unchecked, a Jezebel spirit will drive a person deeper into occult development. This spirit will seek to destroy the pastor's home and the life of a church. Unfortunately, this ravaging pattern of events has been replayed countless times by "the mistress of sorceries, who sells ... families" (Nahum 3:4).

More than likely, you will find believers in your church family who are innocently deceived by these demonic forces. Since they do *not* understand God's Word, they will be unable rightly to discern the spirits that drive them (1 John 4:1; Romans 1:22). Pastors will need to lovingly but firmly confront these individuals. If they do not, Christians under the influence of that spirit will be carried further into greater evil—not to mention the residual effect that will be left in the church for years to come as the following story illustrates.

RESIDENT IN A CHURCH

Glenn attended a spiritually vibrant church. He had an unusual ability to garner sympathy from others. For years, his wife had been sick. Glenn, too, had been fighting various illnesses. However, one never really knew if the illnesses were real or psychosomatic.

Glenn focused his pleas for help on the wealthy members of the church. Out of sympathy, many funneled money to him. Since Glenn was a beloved, grandfatherly figure, many began to believe that Glenn could do no wrong. Even the pastors and elders felt sorry for Glenn. Although they recognized his manipulations, they tolerated them and showed displaced mercy. As a result, a spirit of self-pity and pseudo-spirituality began to spread like a cancer through the Body.

Though this charismatic church embraced the gifts of the Holy Spirit, they became impotent to do the works of the Kingdom. The Jezebel spirit that drove Glenn now became resident within the church. Furthermore, this spirit was seen as a form of godliness. Over time, pastors came and went, battling this unseen, spiritual force. Although the church had been given many prophetic words, God's promises never came to pass due to the weight of this dark spirit.

The Jezebel spirit became a part of the DNA of the church. Although Glenn was later confronted by a pastor, and left the church, taking several families with him, this demonic spirit still remained. Spiritual lethargy permeated the air and a cloak of death filled the atmosphere.

Although a Jezebel spirit likes to attach itself to a person, it can infiltrate and permeate the atmosphere of an entire congregation. Then it will curtail, detour, or even kill prophetic words of invitation to a higher calling for that Body of believers. A lack of confrontation due to unsanctified mercy can influence the spiritual impact of even a mature church. Remember, all unchecked sin will eventually ripen and bring forth fruit that leads to death.

OPERATING THROUGH NON-CHRISTIANS

Many well-meaning believers who operate in a Jezebel spirit may simply need revelation concerning their error. Most likely, this spirit has not fully matured in their life. However, other individuals may resemble the mature Jezebel spirit portrayed in Scripture. Usually these individuals do not know the Lord. They have deliberately joined with a church to destroy it through occult means.

As I have mentioned earlier, we see a clear example of this diabolical scheme in Acts 16. A slave girl who was possessed with a spirit of divination met Paul and Silas on their way to a prayer meeting. Being drawn by their anointing, she began following them announcing, “These men are the servants of the Most High God, who proclaim to us the way of salvation” (Acts 16:17).

The devilish strategy was this: in associating with the apostles, the slave girl would appear to have been “endorsed” by Paul and Silas. Thus, when they continued on their missionary journey, the slave girl would have been positioned to step into prominence. Thereby, Satan would be able to pervert the gifts and callings that Paul had conferred upon the church in Macedonia. By way of deception, the enemy could turn their hearts toward another god, Satan.

BALAAM'S ERROR

Balaam, the soothsayer (Joshua 13:22), also drew upon the occult for revelation and empowerment. In Hebrew, the word "soothsayer" is *quacam,* which means to determine by magical scroll. In using the word soothsayer, Scripture suggests that Balaam perverted his prophetic anointing by practicing the magical arts. Although God spoke to Balaam in the beginning, he later chose to follow darkness, which led to his own demise.

For a hefty reward, Balaam was asked by the messengers of Balak, King of Moab to curse Israel. God had forbidden Balaam to prophesy against Israel. Hoping he could change God's mind, Balaam began to question God. In doing so, he demonstrated his unbroken will, defiance, and insubordination and became increasingly controlling. In this way, he was like Jezebel. He practiced stubborn manipulation and veiled control until he passed the point of no return. As such, Balaam's life manifests the progression of a Jezebel spirit.

ULTERIOR MOTIVES

A subtle distinction exists between entreating God as an intercessor and seeking to override God's commands as a manipulator. A person's motive distinguishes the two. Motive will discern personal gain from corporate gain. Since God is able to search our hearts and discern our motives, He knew that Balaam wanted to manipulate God's laws in order to claim the reward. Balaam's motive was driven by selfish desires.

As an intercessor, Abraham entreated God for the salvation of Sodom and Gomorrah (Genesis 18). Moses, whom God said was the most humble man on the face of the Earth, interceded on behalf of the Hebrew children. Moses asked God to take his life rather than wipe out his countrymen (Exodus 32:32). God heard the cries of both Abraham and Moses and intervened.

Intercession seeks restoration and building up of the things of God. A Jezebel spirit, on the other hand, seeks to unravel and destroy the things of God. Here's the test for all intercessors: God may choose to deny a prayer request for His own reasons. When this happens, how we respond to God's refusal determines everything that follows.

INSUBORDINATION

Wrong responses originate in an attitude of subtle questioning and cajoling. These arise from a heart of insubordination. Just as rebellion is as witchcraft, the Lord says that insubordination is as idolatry (1 Samuel 15:23). In the Hebrew, insubordination means "to push, to press, to urge." A heart of insubordination refuses to be persuaded by those in authority. Individuals with such a heart will distrust, resist, and look for a way to thwart authority. They will do anything to get what they want.

As Scripture records, God played along with Balaam's insubordination (Numbers 22:20). But when God plays along with our game, beware! His judgment is waiting on the threshold.

Although a child may question, urge, and insist on his or her way, this does *not* mean the child has a Jezebel spirit. However, it does indicate that the child is developing a strong will which will need to be corrected. The same is true about a Christian who has an insistent, strong will. Ultimately, the individual will need to be yielded and submitted to the Lord as well as to the spiritual authorities placed over him or her.

DISCERNING MOTIVES

Whenever a motive to usurp authority is discerned, confrontation *must* come from the pastor. A pastor must personally question such individuals and discern their motives. In addition, such confrontations should be done with great gentleness (Galatians 6:1), seeking to avoid putting people in defensive postures. However, be prepared. A person with a Jezebel spirit will try to convince a pastor or leadership that he or she is innocent. They will deny any wrong doing or underhandedness. They will insist their insights and methods are correct. Furthermore, these appeals will usually have a controlling, demanding spirit behind them.

GIVING IMPURELY

When Balaam's questioning did not accomplish his goals, he tried another tactic. He offered a sacrifice to God, hoping God would relent and grant his request (Numbers 23:1-3). Balaam's sacrifice, however, was an attempt to manipulate God. In a similar way, carnally minded individuals may give a gift or a sacrifice to procure God's favor.

When Balaam tried to entice God, it suggested that his heart was hardened and insensitive toward the Lord. Balaam believed that he could wheedle God. He had applied that logic to other gods—evil spirits who had given him knowledge by occult means. Now he was unable to distinguish Jehovah God from other gods. Naturally, Balaam's enticement failed.

A similar fate awaits those operating with a Jezebel spirit. They will sacrifice much, mostly in the eyesight of others. They will dance, cry, raise their hands, fast, and go on various spiritual campaigns in order to move the hand of God. But God's arm will not be twisted by their spiritual ploys. God will not move on behalf of any individual whose motives are impure.

Like Balaam, those with a Jezebel spirit will bait, entice, and sell themselves to obtain power and endorsement. These individuals *must* be confronted during these campaigns and shown their need for repentance.

INTENT TO INJURE

> Look, these women caused the children of Israel, through the counsel of Balaam, to trespass against the Lord in the incident of Peor, and there was a plague among the congregation of the Lord—NUMBERS 31:16.

Balaam's next ploy was manipulation that proved costly to others. Manipulation, in itself, is wrong. Coupled with malice, it becomes evil. When malice is evident, confrontation must occur. According to Webster's Dictionary, to manipulate means "to manage or control artfully or by shrewd use of influence, especially in an unfair or fraudulent way." Manipulation involves skill and influence. It is often used underhandedly or covertly, in order to gain advantage.

Prostituting his prophetic gift by the practice of divination for hire, Balaam manipulated the men of Israel and exploited their weakness by placing beautiful women before them, causing them to stumble sexually. Thereby, the Jews forsook their love of Jehovah God and committed spiritual adultery. Having calculated their downfall, Balaam knew their sexual sin would force God to judge them—creating the same effect as it would had Balaam actually demanded God curse Israel. Hence, Balaam would acquire his reward and Israel would be cursed.

Balaam's heart was hardened to the Lord (Numbers 22:7, 24:1). He was indifferent, cruel, and bitter. Sadly, in the end, Balaam was not remembered as a prophet of God, but as a soothsayer.

MANIPULATION GRIEVES THE HOLY SPIRIT

Most of us can recognize the evil in manipulating others with malice. But someone with a Jezebel spirit may justify evil actions by the supposed good it will eventually bring. The outcome makes no difference—an individual is deceived when he or she uses manipulation, even for the supposed welfare of others.

Unfortunately, many believe they are justified in their actions because they claim "it's for the greater good" of the church. Their logic may sound spiritual, even unselfish, in their own distorted way of thinking. But do not be deceived. Manipulation comes from a wrong spirit. It does *not* reflect submission to God's authority and order. Even if these Christians are in leadership, manipulation by anyone grieves the Holy Spirit.

Although not all manipulation is malicious, it is *always* wrong because it involves setting up people or circumstances to gain desired end results. It is self-serving, even when we think it's for the good of others. Manipulation actually promotes our thoughts above God's thoughts. Whenever we push our ideas ahead of waiting for God to act, we reveal our pride, which is a form of idolatry. Therefore, manipulation must be confronted in the Body of Christ and in personal relationships.

VEILED MANIPULATION

Rick had taken a pastoral position in a church that was known for its compassion to the poor. His church was struggling, and soon he realized why. He discovered that the person who started most of the gossip sat outside his office. His secretary was revealing personal information about everyone who came for counseling, who gave gifts, or who had problems of any kind. After a series of unheeded warnings, Rick had to let her go. While this was done properly, he began hearing rumors of how heartless he had been. Even his elders, who had initially agreed with him, later questioned every decision he made.

Soon, Rick discovered a second problem. His former secretary was a very good friend of the church cleaning woman who had been attending the church for years. The cleaning woman would periodically come up with strange, prophetic-sounding dreams.

Whenever the Holy Spirit would anoint a service, this woman took great delight in telling everyone that she had dreamed about it happening. However, Rick found it hard to keep track of all her dreams and understand how she applied a dream to a particular event. To complicate matters, this woman was in her 60's and used her "prophecies," along with her ill health, to elicit sympathy from others. They, in turn, would feel sorry for her and give her money. In time, this woman became the "real boss" of the church because she had manipulated leadership with her pseudo-spirituality. Whatever she said became the final word! She was also a worse gossiper than Rick's former secretary. Feigning humility, she claimed that she never knew why God would give her these revelations. But none of her prophecies were ever more than fragmentally true, at best.

The turning point came when Rick caught her prophesying about a situation she had discovered by shuffling through papers left on his desk. On this occasion, Rick had forgotten to clear his desk, though that was his usual practice. When she claimed to have received the revelation from God, that was the last straw. Rick let her go and mercifully gave her a month's severance pay. However, she contacted each board member and leader, claiming she was terminated because of her friendship with Rick's former secretary. In a surprising turn of events, the board and leadership insisted that Rick reinstate her. Within a year, Rick left the church and three years after that the church died.

Twisted Thinking

Today, many pastors have felt the effects of a fully developed and demonically empowered Jezebel spirit. Some have had curses placed on them through carnal prayers of well-meaning people, supposedly to accomplish "God's will."

Individuals given to a Jezebel spirit have a conscience that has been seared—calling good "evil" and evil "good." Their speculations have become futile and their hearts have become darkened. Scripture says they are without excuse.

> Thinking themselves to be wise, they became fools—ROMANS 1:20-22.

When an individual given over to a Jezebel spirit reaches this stage of maliciousness, confrontation and removal must occur. The time for repentance has passed.

VIOLENCE AND AGGRESSION

> And she wrote letters in Ahab's name, sealed them with his seal, and sent letters to the elders and the nobles who were dwelling in the city with Naboth. She wrote in the letters, saying 'Proclaim a fast, and seat Naboth with high honor among the people; and seat two men, scoundrels, before him, saying, 'You have blasphemed God and the king.' Then take him out, and stone him, that he may die—1 KINGS 21:8-10.

In this biblical account, Jezebel proclaimed a fast and planted false witnesses to achieve her objectives. Similarly, someone given over to a Jezebel spirit may use spiritual disciplines while stirring up accusations designed to support his or her cause. This may take the form of verbal malice or even overt forms of hostility. These attacks increase in intensity toward the intended victim, as demonic spirits empower the Jezebelite. Such actions indicate deeply rooted animosity and hatred toward those who disagree with a Jezebelite's will and desires.

In the end, individuals fully given over to a Jezebel spirit malign, disgrace, and seek to destroy a person's influence. They do this by speaking evil of their victim's spirituality and attempting to destroy the person's influence. Jezebel illustrated this when she seized Naboth's vineyard. Scripture reveals the strength of her malice and the extent of her violence and aggression.

Individuals given over to a Jezebel spirit may confine their actions to emotional, verbal, or mental abuse. They may explode with rage and with vengeance. However, they justify their ruthless actions by continuing to believe that the end result justifies the means.

Murderous Rage

Jezebel plotted to frame Naboth and then kill him—all in the proper religious forms of the day—since he refused to sell his vineyard to Ahab who coveted it. Before his leaders and his neighbors, she coerced two false witnesses to accuse Naboth of cursing God. Then she compelled the elders of Israel to comply with the Law and stone him. Although she was "religious," she was guilty of murder, which is an evil tool to subjugate the will of someone else.

In essence, Jezebel's greatest act of control was murdering someone—whether it was Naboth or the hundreds of God's prophets—to acquire what you wanted. Balaam, too, brought about the destruction of many by his shrewdness. Both Balaam and Jezebel were executed by a kingly figure: Balaam was slain at the command of Moses and Jezebel was killed at the command of Jehu.

So it must be with the Church today. A pastor must not allow innocent people to be injured or destroyed by someone's lust for power and control. The Jezebel spirit cannot be tolerated in the Body of Christ. Pastoral leadership *must* remove this dark influence in their church.

This principle is exactly what the apostle Paul ordered the Church in Corinth to do, when he admonished them to cast out the young man who was sexually involved with his stepmother (1 Corinthians 5). The dark spirit would infect the entire church.

PRACTICED SKILLS

Individuals with a Jezebel spirit are skilled in getting their way. They may use strategies of flattery, persuasion, sexual seduction, slander, lying, accusation, intimidation, secrecy, persecution, framing another person for a wrong done, or generating emotional and/or spiritual dependency in someone.

Such individuals are driven by jealousy, rivalry, elitism, and a need to self-promote, dominate, and monopolize someone's time and attention. Furthermore, these individuals will malign anyone who gets in their way.

When left unchecked, the Jezebel spirit will cause some people to actively pursue one leader after another, each time stating their case to gain acceptance. Like rebellious children going from one parent to the other, Jezebelites search out others to agree with their grievances. They will seek to influence others to heed their selfish demands. If a situation is not resolved to their satisfaction, Jezebel will malign—insinuate, badmouth, smear—their target and plant libelous doubts in the minds of others. They will also coyly violate disciplinary instructions, in an attempt to garner misguided sympathy and support. This tactic seems to satiate Jezebel's false sense of justice.

Jealousy

A spirit of jealousy plays a key role in fueling a Jezebel spirit. Jealousy seeks to monopolize the attention, admiration, or energy of its subjects. When coupled with control, a person driven by jealousy will seek to eliminate any competition.

A Jezebelite is always threatened by gifted prophetic people, because through revelation a Jezebelite's cloaked schemes are revealed. A prophetic intercessor whose prayer can depose a Jezebelite's powerbase is likewise a formidable foe. Thus, a Jezebelite despises authentic intercessory prayer and anointed prophetic ministries. True prophetic anointing manifests God-ordained spiritual authority. A Jezebelite, who seeks to control others, will be frustrated by godly authority and threatened by those to whom it is entrusted.

Accusation

Accusation is another common tool used by an individual with a Jezebel spirit. When this spirit is fully developed, demons assist the person to intimidate and induce fear in others.

Accusation's power is satanic. It sows fear in an individual's heart. It causes people to run. Satan is the accuser of the brethren (Revelation 12:10), as well as the father of lies. A spirit of accusation has no truthful rationale behind it. Therefore, it cannot be reasoned with. It can only be dealt with as the Holy Spirit enlightens those in leadership. As with Korah, there will always be something to camouflage the real issue, which is a spirit of lawlessness.

Those who walk in an accusing spirit are actually agreeing with the doctrine of demons. Therefore, God will hold them accountable, no matter what situation they are trying to correct. This is why the apostle James says that wherever you find slander and accusation, there also exists every evil thing (James 3:16).

An accusing spirit also works hand-and-glove with a religious spirit. Together, they become a formidable and unrighteous force at work in a church, forging a critical base of support for Satan's cause.

Pastors and leaders who seek to deal with a Jezebel spirit should be aware of operating in an accusing spirit. If a pastor or leader brings a charge against a Jezebelite, it must be based on factual evidence supported by witnesses. Unwise accusations, on the other hand, are based on supposition—what you believe is going on. Improper accusations are fueled by fear and will only result in denial and a "kickback" of charges in retaliation against a pastor, causing a pastor to lose favor with leadership.

CHAPTER 9

THE HEART OF THE MATTER

By all appearances, Brenda and Brad were a successful young couple. They dressed impeccably, were athletic, and drove BMWs. After becoming Christians, they channeled their ambitious drives for success into becoming deeply involved in a local church. They became active in various ministries, holding dinners and prayer meetings. Their winsome and outgoing personalities attracted many. It seemed they were born for ministry. Not long thereafter, Brenda and Brad gained the attention of Henry, the senior pastor. A bond of friendship grew. In time, Brad became Henry's associate pastor. But trouble was brewing under the surface.

On the outside, Brenda and Brad seemed to have the perfect marriage. Brad was poised and strong, but through his new position, Brenda was slowly becoming more intimidating. She could be emotionally overwhelming. After Brad had been four years on staff, the pastor began to notice that Brenda's opinions now seemed to overrule

Brad's wishes. He would simply cave into Brenda's strong and unflinching will.

Just as she had done with Brad, Brenda began to exert her strong will toward Henry. If she was not given a position for which she had lobbied, Brenda would pout and vent her disappointment. This unchecked rebellion was now turning into anger and bitterness. Although she maintained a face of compliance in front of Henry, she began to spread lies, saying he had a deep-seeded hatred of women. Although she had never approached Henry about her feelings, he had begun to hear rumors of what was being said behind his back.

On several occasions, Henry approached Brad about the rumors. This strategy seemed to quiet Brenda, but the calm was only momentary. Periodically, Brenda's anger would explode in staff meetings. During those times, she would confront Henry in a hostile and derogatory way. Soon, Brenda was meeting privately with other leader's wives and stirring up dissension. Two staff members resigned as a result.

From behind the scenes, Brenda had hoped to stage a coup and instate Brad as the senior pastor. She believed he would make a much better pastor than Henry. However before this could happen, the people began to scatter and run. Half the church left. Then, just when Brenda sensed the ruse was up and Henry was aware that she was the real problem, she convinced Brad to resign. Sadly, Brad never realized what his wife had done.

GESTATION TIME

As seen in this story, a Jezebel spirit matures over time. This developmental process involves individuals gradually accepting demonically inspired thoughts. Over time, these thoughts become justified in their minds and lead them to take actions which they believe are from God.

As this spirit matures, it will bring forth an abundance of prickly, poisonous, and deadly fruit, which is often disguised as enticing and spiritual. Those who reach for this fruit are pricked by hidden thorns, causing them to bleed, and are poisoned once they eat of its fruit.

COUNTERFEIT VOICES

The Jezebel spirit is a treacherous impostor within the Church. It counterfeits the true prophetic gift, and it imitates and maligns the proper function of prophetic ministries. Other darker counterfeits to the prophetic—psychics, clairvoyants, palm-readers who practice witchcraft, divination, and sorcery—have arisen to speak about the supernatural. However, a Jezebel spirit is more deceptive, simply because it is less obvious to the untrained eye, and it parades on scriptural grounds.

Although an individual given over to a Jezebel spirit may not practice the black arts or the deep secrets of Satan, they share the same clandestine, demonic roots with those in the occult. In fact, individuals controlled by a Jezebel spirit often bear greater fruit, because their actions are more covert and their roots become more entrenched before becoming detected.

Every church that embraces a prophetic ministry will have to contend with the Jezebel spirit because this demonic spirit mimics the prophetic gifts and callings of God. This spirit actually comes to destroy the prophetic gift. Consequently, it works covertly and its activities are extremely treacherous.

Individuals given over to this spirit often try to enhance and strengthen their powerbase by attracting and controlling others, acting much like a spiritual magnet. Pastors and leaders will need to recognize the working of this covert spirit because it will seek to divide groups and stir up contention, confusion, and deception in the Church.

ALLOWANCES FOR THE IMMATURE

A clear distinction must be made between an immature prophetic person and someone who has a Jezebel spirit. Those who are prophetically immature are merely trying to find their rightful place in the Body. They may lack wisdom and humility, however their intention is *not* to destroy the church. Overly eager and immature prophetic individuals will do things that seem foolish or unwise. But just as we don't kill our children for their immaturity, neither should we kill those who are in prophetic infancy. Pastors and leaders must make allowances for a young prophetic individual's childishness. Pastors and leaders must overcome their weariness of having young prophets who need to be trained.

As we—in the wisdom and counsel of the Lord—sharpen and hone the skills of those with prophetic gifts, it will bring forth valor and purity in the prophetic ministry. Eventually, such individuals will bring insight, revelation, and wisdom to the Body of Christ. Thus, all the petty difficulties of this gestation period will seem worth the time and effort expended.

During this developmental season, it's especially important *not* to maim or abort the gifts of young prophetic

Christians by accusing them of having a Jezebel spirit. Pastors and leaders must learn to discern how to bring correction and how to nurture budding prophetic gifts, without wounding or killing people's spirits.

Sometimes the difference between an immature prophetic person and someone who operates with an immature Jezebel spirit is very subtle. To discern the difference involves looking at the heart of the matter. A young prophetic person begins with a heart to serve God. Those operating with a Jezebel spirit may have started out with a heart to serve God, but at some point they have departed from that path into one of self-promotion. Several additional points of departure are described more fully below.

1. SELFISH AMBITION

As Scripture advises us:

> Let nothing be done through selfish ambition or conceit, but in lowliness of mind let each of you esteem others better than himself—PHILIPPIANS 2:3.

Individuals with a Jezebel spirit, loving the acclaim of others, will often give themselves a title or seek after a leadership position. Demonstrating elitism, they will regard a certain position as being "the most anointed" and dismiss another as being "less anointed" or as not having a voice in the church or in spiritual matters.

They will become zealous to market their gifts and broaden their sphere of influence. Often such individuals will not consult the Lord about where and when to minister.

They will simply yield to the need for greater press. As their success increases, they will run to deliver many words, although God has not sent them. They may even believe that as their reputation increases, God's Kingdom will also increase. However, they are sadly deceived.

On the other hand, young prophetic individuals may gravitate initially toward the distinction thrust on them. But as they mature, most will shun any fanfare or publicity. They will realize that being in the limelight only serves to blind their eyes to God's high calling and that fame actually detracts from spending time alone with the Lord.

Individuals who are called to prophetic ministry must also desire to be held accountable for their words and actions. They should welcome others pointing out their errors and weaknesses. They must learn to submit to spiritual authority. One of the hallmarks of those with the heart of God is how they respond to correction. Those with a Jezebel spirit chafe when corrected, but those operating under the Holy Spirit will repent.

In the process of submission, they learn to die to self-will. This is an incredibly painful process, but all of us must pay the price and crucify our soul, as well as our fleshly desires. Willingness to submit every aspect of life and ministry to the Lord must be evident in those who stand to lead His Church.

2. Personal Gain

While a prophetic person goes through a costly breaking process (Nehemiah 5:14-19), an individual with a Jezebelite rarely makes such sacrifices. For the most part, a Jezebelite will express a persistent drive to demonstrate his or her "prophetic insight." In doing so, he or she has an ulterior motive and will insist upon some sort of payback—recognition, fame, money, clothing, or various privileges lavished upon him or her by individuals easily infatuated with supernatural insight.

Quickly, this self-centered individual will notice their prophetic insight can open doors. Consequently, he or she will give into the temptation to use their gift, mixed with human prognostication and personal opinion. Such an individual may read people's souls and later present their soulish insight as divinely inspired prophecy. When this tainted revelation comes forth, it will lead astray those who are not in tune with the Holy Spirit. So while the Jezebel spirit seeks to tear apart, the prophetic ministry seeks to serve and to encourage others and leave the hearer with a sense of hope.

3. A Lust for Life

Sensual appetites will often run rampant in individuals who operate with a Jezebel spirit. A spirit of lust will eat away at their soul, until it gains control of them. Such lust is not simply sexually oriented. Money, favor, or recognition may feed their ambition and offer desired results. An insatiable thirst for self-indulgent pleasures will grow. Conversely, the work of the Cross will cease to be manifested in this person's life.

4. Demonic Entanglement

As individuals approach an intermediate level of demonic entanglement, their purposes will become more cunning and deliberate. These individuals will try to control the actions of friends, families, and churches. Whenever false humility, lies, and flattery do not bring about the expected esteem and recognition, these individuals often resort to anger, condemnation, accusation, and domination.

Over time, such individuals will become increasingly more problematic. They will have become quite skilled and able to rationalize their brusque behavior with confusing spiritual language. Those who attempt to confront them without being prepared will walk away scratching their heads in confusion and will dismiss the thought that the person had Jezebellic tendencies—even though their initial discernment was correct.

If their strong will and insubordination are not dealt with, Jezebelites will rebel against any authority that does not agree with them. In addition, they will counsel others to rebel against pastoral authority—often presenting those who disagree with them as being spiritually blind or naive. This unchecked rebellion will open the door for other evil spirits to infiltrate them, their followers, or even an entire church. Consequently, a sudden, violent verbal attack may arise and be specifically targeted toward individuals who do not show loyalty or submission to the Jezebelite. Meanwhile, church members who seem indifferent or complacent to this rebellion will end up serving as pawns in a demonic game of win or lose. Tragically, the end result will usually be a church split.

5. A Spirit of Lawlessness

Lawlessness is a term used to describe people who are not restrained or controlled by the law, especially God's Word. In essence, all rebellion against God is lawlessness (1 John 3:4). Those who were responsible for the death of Jesus are characterized as lawless (Acts 2:23). The leader of the end-time rebellion, the Antichrist, is called the man of lawlessness (2 Thessalonians 2).

A spirit of lawlessness unleashes its attack on the Kingdom of God and drives individuals to rebel and oppose God's appointed leaders. This spirit inspires innuendoes, rumors, lies, slander, manipulation, and control by creating schisms—or threatening to do so. Thus, whoever covertly challenges and slanders godly pastors and other ministries has violated God's established rules for His Kingdom. Such thinking is rebellion or sin.

> Whoever commits sin also commits *lawlessness*, and sin is *lawlessness*—1 John 3:4.

Our omniscient God has foreknowledge of each pastor's theology, gifts, experiences, and personality. With infinite insight, God knows exactly how a pastor will carry out his or her ideas and plans for a church. A pastor's strengths will probably be evidenced first, followed by their weaknesses—neither of which surprise God. Thus, a pastor known to hurt people in relationships, whether knowingly or unknowingly, continues to be allowed to lead a church in spite of his or her weaknesses. God is patient, watching faithful pastors mature in character and gifting. Therefore if your pastor offends you, could it be God is using him or her to reveal your heart?

Proper Protocol

By speaking against God's established leaders, you are sowing seeds for your own destruction. Remember, Scripture tells us:

> Do not receive an accusation against an elder except from two or three witnesses—1 TIMOTHY 5:19.

The passage in Matthew 18 provides us with proper protocol to follow with any church member, including a pastor or a leader who has sinned or is in error.

> Moreover if your brother sins against you, go and tell him his fault between you and him alone. If he hears you, you have gained your brother. But if he will not hear, take with you one or two more, that 'by the mouth of two or three witnesses every word may be established.' And if he refuses to hear them, tell it to the church. But if he refuses even to hear the church, let him be to you like a heathen and a tax collector—Matthew 18:15-18.

Even if your pastor is angry and controlling like Saul, you *must* demonstrate a heart of David. You must refrain from taking the opportunity to "kill" God's leader (1 Samuel 24). David waited for God to intervene and deal with Saul. May it never be said of you, as it was of Absalom, that you stole the hearts of the people away from your pastor (2 Samuel 15:4-6).

Let God judge your pastor. If you judge him or her, God will be justified in saying, "Since men have taken action, I will step back." Thus, God will allow us to live with the results of our actions. In addition, by taking judgement into our own hands, we give demonic spirits a legal right to judge, hassle, harass, and come against us, simply because we have acted presumptively and have stepped out from under our covering. Therefore, it would be better to leave a church quietly than to speak against God's anointed.

Some people erroneously think that because their gifts continue to be used, their actions are sanctioned by God. Remember what the Lord said:

> Not everyone who says to Me, 'Lord, Lord,' shall enter the kingdom of heaven, but he who does the will of My Father in heaven. Many will say to Me in that day, 'Lord, Lord, have we not prophesied in Your name, cast out demons in Your name, and done many wonders in Your name?' And then I will declare to them, 'I never knew you; depart from Me, you who practice *lawlessness*!'—MATTHEW 7:21-23.

Some of us may think that because we are casting out demons, healing the sick, raising the dead, or prophesying accurately that it indicates God's stamp of approval.We may think we are within the will of God when we criticize our pastor, but God calls it lawlessness.

As Jesus once said, "These people draw near to Me with their mouth, and honor Me with their lips, but their heart is far from Me" (Matthew 15:8). A heart dedicated and consecrated to the Lord honors the spiritual authority that God has established. A heart that rejects that authority allows lawlessness to influence perceptions and decisions.

Please understand that I am not saying we cannot question a spiritual leader who has authority over us. Inquiry is an important process of maturity. However, what we do after a disagreement is critical. If our conversation becomes covert, hidden, and malicious, then we are treading in the realm of lawlessness. Our actions depict lawlessness, especially if our intent is to remove that leader. It would be wise to remember that in the *Didache* or writings of the Early Church fathers, there were only four reasons that warranted removing a pastor. Those were moral failure; financial impropriety; teaching heresy; rage or uncontrolled emotions.

THE MYSTERY OF DECEPTION

> For the *mystery of lawlessness* is already at work; only He who now restrains will do so until He is taken out of the way—2 THESSALONIANS 2:7.

The word *mystery* is defined by Webster as "a religious truth that one can know only by revelation." Thus, the mystery of lawlessness will involve the condition of being deceived. When individuals are involved in lawless acts, they are often unaware of being in rebellion. They are misled by a mental stronghold of self-righteous thinking and are fooled into thinking they are doing God—and the church—a favor. Thus, they have elevated their way of thinking and are trying to correct someone God has chosen as their authority. Their actions demonstrate that they actually despise authority.

The mystery of lawlessness has been and is still powerfully at work in our culture. Satan has subtly persuaded many to embrace relativism—a theory that ethical truths are defined by individuals, groups, circumstances, and situations. Today, many believe there are no universal absolutes. Each person defines his or her rules. Many believe that "what's right for one person is not right for another." Tolerance becomes the cultural buzzword meant to disarm anyone who embraces biblical absolutes.

People who are deceived by lawlessness do not understand that by rejecting God's laws they are led into even greater licentiousness and enslavement to sin. When lawlessness is practiced, it becomes easier to do it again. Thus, lawlessness leads to more lawlessness.

> I speak in human terms because of the weakness of your flesh. For just as you presented your members as slaves of uncleanness, and of *lawlessness* leading to more *lawlessness*, so now present your members as slaves of righteousness for holiness—ROMANS 6:19.

Over the years I have found that many who try to remove a pastor in one church will repeat their actions in another church. They develop a history of causing church problems. I have also discovered that churches launched from a church split often end up splitting themselves. In these situations, the spirit of Jezebel flourishes.

In Scripture, the spirit of lawlessness is linked to the spirit of lust or uncleanness, which corrupt the soul. Those who practice lawlessness walk according to their own ungodly lusts. Scripture calls them "sensual persons" (Jude 19).

Lawlessness results in unfruitfulness and unanswered prayers. It causes us to ask amiss and for personal benefit (James 4:3). Lawlessness causes us to curse men whom God has made, inferring that God was unaware of whom He was making.

> With [the tongue] we bless our God...and with it we curse men, who have been made in the similitude of God—JAMES 3:9.

Throughout Scripture, we are exhorted *not* to live according to this world, but to pursue peace with all men (Hebrews 12:14). We must also treat authority figures with respect (Romans 13:1-7). When we do, God will anoint us with the oil of gladness and with eternal life (Psalm133).

God gives us the choice of becoming a vessel of honor or of dishonor—to be mightily used of God or to be cast away from His presence (2 Timothy 2:20-21). Our willingness to choose obedience, in the midst of disagreement, is *key* to walking as a vessel of honor.

> He who keeps His command will experience nothing harmful; and a wise man's heart discerns both time and procedure, because for every matter there is a time and procedure, though the misery of man increases greatly—ECCLESIASTES 8:5-6, NASB.

A CORRECT RESPONSE TO AUTHORITY

Since God has placed those in authority over us, we must be willing to submit to them. We should also make it a joy for them to watch over our souls.

> Obey those who rule over you... Let them do so with joy and not with grief, for that would be unprofitable for you—HEBREWS 13:17-18.

Your willingness to submit to those in authority does not mean that you cannot have different ideas. You can experience great diversity in the midst of great unity. Once a course of action has been taken by leadership, however, you need to support their decision. If you find yourself questioning the direction taken by leadership, then seek another church that lines up with your ideals and calling. Furthermore, when making that change, do so with grace and humility, *not* with discord or strife. Otherwise, Scripture says it will be "unprofitable" for you.

> The king's heart is in the hand of the Lord,
> like the rivers of water; He turns it wherever
> He wishes—Proverbs 21:1.

As you examine your own heart, ask yourself: Do you *really* believe God can turn your pastor's heart? Then why not step back and pray? We serve a faithful and just God, who is capable of bringing about changes in the heart of your pastor. If God shares your beliefs and priorities for the church, you may witness the pastor responding to divine revelation, which affects a change in his or her decisions and actions. If God does not bring about the changes you desire, perhaps the more important issue is you, not your pastor! Then you may want to ask yourself, "What is God trying to change in me?"

Accepting honest answers to questions such as these may point out areas in your life in which God desires change. In this process, you may benefit from a deeper understanding of yourself. You will also grow closer to the Lord, as you look to Him to influence your pastor.

SOME BASIC ASSUMPTIONS

Before going further, you may want to consider the following presuppositions:

PREMISE 1: Our heavenly Father is infinitely wise and insightful. His knowledge is complete and extends to the past, present, and future.

PREMISE 2: God establishes *all* authority in its position.

PREMISE 3: God allowed the decisions to happen that placed your pastor in your church, knowing exactly what he or she would do.

PREMISE 4: Having infinite awareness, God is *not* surprised by what your pastor is, or is not, doing.

PREMISE 5: As all powerful, God can cause your pastor to stop any course of action, should the Lord choose. He could visit your pastor and tell him or her to stop, if God thought it was important to do so.

PREMISE 6: Perhaps if God is not correcting your pastor, then He may be using the situation to work in your life, as well as in the life of your pastor.

PREMISE 7: Assuming that God is working in your life and in your pastor's life, then it would be wise to remember the words of Jesus: Blessed are the merciful, for they shall receive mercy (Matthew 5:7). In showing mercy to your pastor, you will receive mercy from God.

PREMISE 8: To challenge pastoral authority (except for the four issues of moral failure, financial impropriety, teaching heresy, rage or uncontrolled emotions) is to act presumptively as though you are God. The consequences of such behavior may be grave.

CHAPTER 10

PREPARING TO MINISTER TO THE WOUNDED

IN THE SHORT SPAN of two years, Joel watched his church shrink to less than half its size. During that time, he noticed a woman who embodied what any pastor would have been thrilled to see in a church member—someone who seemed supportive, humble, prayerful, and sincere. One Saturday morning, however, Joel's eyes were painfully opened.

The woman, who was a divorcée, arrived at a couple's marriage retreat and forcibly tried to take over the microphone during one session. Joel could not figure out what had come over her. A few weeks later, his reservations about the woman were fortified when he opened the mail and found a letter from the woman's friend. Worded as if God had dictated the letter, the writer said the divorcée was Joel's true spiritual mate and strongly insinuated that he should leave his wife, who was "holding him back spiritually." Since the divorcée did not actually write the letter, Joel was confused about how to confront this attack on his marriage.

One morning after a prayer meeting, he was having coffee with a small group that included the divorcée. She offered some "directions from God." When he did not accept them, she became angry. Her emotions escalated within minutes. Suddenly she slammed her fist down on the table, spilling cups of coffee, and left.

A few weeks later, when a prophetic ministry came to the church for a conference, the prophet gave a word to the pastor. He warned about a so-called "spiritual mate" who was trying to rise up in the church. Surprised by the revelation, Joel spoke privately to the woman about this prophetic word. The following day in church, the divorcée stood and walked to the front, calmly and firmly interrupting the prophet who was speaking. Cloaked in false humility, she read a written and slanderous rebuke. By that time, the pastor had enough. He told the divorcée she was wrong in her assessment and he wanted to see her in his office the next day. But she never showed up. She left the church, but the damage had been done. Within a year, the church died.

APPRAISE THE CONDITION OF YOUR HEART

Confronting this spirit is not as easy as it may seem. It is hard to diagnose, due to its many faces. One minute, it can appear prayerfully submissive and the next it can act bold and brash. Or it may simply appear to be concerned for the well-being of the church. Like an octopus with eight spindly arms, this spirit is a nightmare to dislodge.

Before confronting someone with a Jezebel spirit, a pastor must first assess his or her own personal and spiritual condition. Danger lies in being tempted to react defensively and to misuse your power.

If a pastor feels intimidated by previous encounters with a Jezebel spirit, future scenarios may leave him or her feeling bitter, resentful, and angry. If these feelings exist, it simply signals that the pastor is not ready to effectively deal with this spirit. Before going further, the pastor may need to appoint someone with wisdom, discernment, and spiritual authority, as well as a "eunuch mentality" to help. This may require that a pastor look for a specialist in deliverance ministry. There are a growing number of ministries that specialize in such concerns as this.

Those who are going to address the Jezebel spirit operating through a person must first pause and assess their own spiritual condition. Ask yourself: Are you feeling any jealousy, strife, envy, or malice toward a past or present authority figure in your life? Do you harbor any hidden feelings of rejection or being overlooked?

Such feelings may lead you to overreact to the Jezebel spirit. Until these attitudes are overcome, addressing a spirit of insubordination and rebellion in another cannot be fully or powerfully accomplished. In addition, there are other issues to be dealt with.

Deal with Your Frustration

> ...you who are spiritual restore such a one in a spirit of gentleness, considering yourself lest you also be tempted—Galatians 6:1.

If a pastor has not dealt immediately with each issue that has arisen, they must deal with their frustration and anger that may have mounted. Frankly, no one likes to be controlled by another person. If a pastor has been wounded by someone with a Jezebel spirit, then he or she is an ideal candidate for mishandling a ministry situation. Scripture warns us:

> For the wrath of man does not produce the righteousness of God—JAMES 1:20.

Since an individual with a Jezebel spirit often uses criticism and accusation, such demonic spirits cannot be driven out by a pastor who reacts in like manner. A pastor must first confront and deal with his or her own critical and accusing spirit.

DO NOT RETALIATE

When control and manipulation are evidenced in a pastor's life, he or she will become defenseless against a Jezebel spirit. In counteracting manipulation with manipulation, the pastor will have failed to walk in the fruit of the Holy Spirit. Moreover, God does *not* honor our actions when we return evil for evil.

Whenever we retaliate this way, our anger has twice the impact. First, we lash out because we are angry with ourselves for allowing the wound to remain in our soul. Second, we react because we are angry with the person who manifests the same propensity toward sin. We are often guilty of attacking the very weaknesses in others that are evidenced in our lives.

When pastors feel insecure or uncertain of how to handle a situation, they may resort to intimidation. They do this to maintain control. Intimidation, however, will never bring true repentance or restoration, which should *always* be our goal. Intimidation will only produce a temporary remorse, feigned repentance, or withdrawal. Consequently, intimidation will abort any sincere opportunity to minister healing to a wounded person.

Attempting to create fear in someone else by appearing more powerful will only complicate the problem. It will drive a pastor to badger, belittle, and attempt to "back the person into a corner." Such methods will only birth more hostility. Or it will provoke the individual to stir up slander or plan acts of violence and rage.

When a pastor reacts to a Jezebelite in anger, the Jezebelite will begin to appear to cower. Such individuals will portray themselves as being a victim and you as being an ogre. This usually happens whenever others are present to witness your angry outburst, which will make it seem as if the Jezebelite is the underdog. If you haven't already experienced this, you will. It is only a matter of time.

Check the Mirror

Instinctively, individuals with a Jezebel spirit will often mirror a pastor's manner of operation. If the pastor is self-promoting, such individuals may feel the freedom to promote their own gifts and abilities. If the leader is domineering, individuals may see this as granting permission to maintain the upper hand at all times with others. If a domineering pastor clashes with such strong-willed Jezebels, a fierce and ugly battle will arise.

I recommend that a pastor focus his or her attention on opposing the demonic stronghold in the person while demonstrating love toward the person. Any confrontation must be done in love in order to restore the Jezebelite. Only a loving confrontation will induce an individual to experience brokenness. He or she will need to experience godly sorrow that leads to repentance.

If you face resistance by the Jezebelite, avoid the tendency to react scornfully. Remember, you are *not* wrestling against flesh and blood, but against the powers of darkness (Ephesians 6:12). Ask God to search your heart further. Then respond with great strength and determination to help the individual repent. If you are defensive or reactive, the Jezebelite may detect your insecurity and respond with a mask of meekness meant to disarm you. Your confidence must be in the Lord. Believing that God has appointed you as shepherd over the flock will enable you to act valiantly and with compassion.

GUARD AGAINST TRANSFERENCE

Memories of neglect from a mother, from prior romantic relationships, or from fluctuations in a marriage influence a pastor's ability to communicate and confront. Jezebelites will usually sense a pastor's bitterness or areas of unresolved wounds. Therefore, a pastor must guard against transferring unconscious and unsettled issues about a grandmother, mother, sister, or spouse to individuals operating under a Jezebel spirit.

Suspicion, strife, and vain imagination about potential conflicts will tempt a pastor to eradicate anyone who seems unsubmissive. However suspicion, strife, and vain imagination are spirits of witchcraft. If a pastor is tempted to operate in these ways, such spirits may obtain a foothold in him or her. A pastor will *not* be able to overcome a Jezebel spirit until freed of these heart issues. Furthermore, demonic spirits may attack a pastor or leader who arrogantly or smugly attacks a Jezebel spirit.

To operate in the wrong spirit is sometimes described as operating in the power of the soul. Whenever we use our soul to conquer another's soul, we fail to get God's needed counsel to gain victory. Only by exercising the fruits of the Holy Spirit—love, joy, peace, longsuffering, kindness, goodness, faithfulness, gentleness, and self-control —can the power of the soul be conquered. Remember, a spiritual touch can produce eternal change in another. Trying to use the soul in this manner will bring disaster to a pastor, his or her family, and the church.

A pastor must keep in mind that he or she is dealing with dark powers. This battle is not merely with a person. The enemy's success distorts our thinking and produces a spirit of fear, suspicion, or accusation in our hearts. The Jezebel spirit operates under the power of the soul. If you operate under the same power, you inflate the demonic spirit and it now controls both of you.

A TRAGIC ENCOUNTER

Shortly after his fortieth birthday, Martin was meeting with a couple from his church. He was convinced they operated with a Jezebel spirit. It was their second meeting and Martin had invited the elders. Although the first meeting had been volatile, Martin was prepared for this confrontation. He was determined the couple would not make him look bad, although they had threatened to do so.

Secretly, Martin hated confrontation. He avoided it. But he remembered two other occasions when he had failed to address this issue and the results had been devastating—two church splits. The last one had cost Martin his position at a large prestigious church in another state. Martin made a resolve that he would never let such a thing happen again. He would snuff out any nonsense before it got worse. Tonight, the elders would witness this couple's hostile personal agenda just as he had in their previous meeting.

Two hours later, Martin sat with his face buried in his hands. He was deeply frustrated. Nothing had changed. No admission of guilt had been made by the couple. Furthermore, they showed no remorse for their actions. Instead, they acted coy and innocent. They even accused Martin of misunderstanding their words and actions.

During the meeting, the couple often said they were *only* trying to serve God. With tears running down their faces, they reminded Martin and the elders of all the times they had helped him and the church. Soft-spoken and seemingly humble, the couple questioned Martin's motives and claimed he was turning a molehill into a mountain.

They had turned the tables on Martin. Listening to them, Martin even became confused and began to wonder if they were right. Perhaps his own fear and insecurity drove him to point his finger at them.

After the couple left, the elders further probed Martin about his accusations. They began to side with the couple. They also speculated about the reason for Martin's charges. Martin saw doubt creep into their faces. They were puzzled about his discernment and leadership skills.

Three months later, the couple stood up during the church service and demanded Martin's resignation. They listed their reasons and worded their accusations as if God had spoken. When Martin refused to resign, they shouted, "Ichabod," meaning "the glory has departed from Israel". Then, they marched out of the church. Eighty church members filed out with them. Two months later, Martin took a sabbatical. Sadly, he never returned to the ministry again.

WHEN MINISTERING TO OTHERS

You will need to encourage a person who has repented from using a Jezebel spirit to continue taking new steps forward. He or she must be encouraged to keep renewing his or her mind, learning to recognize and adopt God's way of looking at things.

Activities that restore feelings of self-worth should be encouraged. Frequently, these individuals have a great desire to contribute in a worthwhile way. Servanthood, with healthy boundaries, is a key to restoration. However, their serving others should not be confused with their having authority. To give them authority at this time would be tantamount to giving an alcoholic a drink.

All areas of rebellion will need to be addressed. In an attitude of meekness, amends will need to be made in order to close the door to future inroads by the enemy.

SUGGESTED STEPS FOR CONFRONTATION

For pastors who must confront an individual who operates with a Jezebel spirit, here are my suggestions:

1. Seek counsel about any personal blind spots or weaknesses you have from those who are spiritually mature.
2. Pray before you speak in any confrontation. Ask the Holy Spirit to reveal hidden issues. If you allow the Holy Spirit to do His work, it is amazing how issues will surface that had not been previously known.
3. Ask the Holy Spirit for wisdom to discern what is spiritual, by discerning what demonic spirits the individual has embraced. Ask for discernment about what is natural or from the person's upbringing, such as harsh parental issues.
4. Avoid becoming angry at all costs! Keep calm. Do not overreact or make the issue larger than it is.
5. Do not ignore the problem! It will *not* disappear.
6. From the moment a problem is suspected, document all third-party information. Record dates, times, places, and what was said. Otherwise, trying to piece together tidbits of information will only lead to the person's denial.
7. During a confrontation, *always* have someone in the room with you.
8. Confront each issue with grace, but with firmness and candor. Be specific. You must explain the problems. However do not make the mistake of revealing names and specific accusations.
9. Get permission from third parties to use all testimonies, along with their names, in the meeting. If you do not, the Jezebelite will deny ever having said such things.

10. Tape record the meeting. Be sure to let the individual know that you are taping the meeting. Set the tape recorder in the open for all to see.

If you follow these suggestions, be prepared for Jezebel to repent and apologize with great passion. However, do not be surprised when Jezebel, whom you thought had repented, recoils and strikes again with greater vengeance. If that happens, simply repeat the above process of confrontation. If the person will not hear you the second time, then you *must* remove him or her from the church.

RED FLAGS

Here are some early warning signs that pastors, in hindsight, have shared with me. Pastors may want to keep alert for these phrases that *could* indicate a storm is brewing on the horizon.

1. "I just want to be your friend." More than likely, people who say these things will have expectations that you will never be able to meet.

2. "I just want to help you get to where God has called you." In other words, "you cannot get to your destiny without me." Beware!

3. "There are no strings attached to my help. I just want to serve." However, you'll find lots of hidden strings.

4. "You can trust me. I will always support you." Such people will support you as long as you do what they say!

5. "You do not acknowledge my gifting." People like this are asking you for more authority in the church.

6. "You do not understand me." This is a veiled cry for you to spend more time with them than you have available.

7. "You intimidate me. I do not feel like I can talk to you." In other words, "My goals should become your goals."

8. "I have new revelation. The pastor has Old Testament understanding and I have New Testament understanding." In other words, "I am right and you are wrong!"

9. "The Lord has given me some things that I need to share with you." Duck! You'll probably be receiving a harsh spanking.

10. "My last pastor did not know how to use me or my gifts." In other words, they are saying, "Let me have my way."

FOR OUR GOOD

If handled rightly, an attack by a Jezebel spirit will ultimately strengthen a church. God uses the fiery battles of life to train, strengthen, and refine us (1 Peter 4:12-19). As God once told me: Small battles produce small victories, but great battles produce great victories—in our lives, in our ministries, and in our churches.

CHAPTER 11

DISMANTLING JEZEBEL'S MANTLE

JEREMIAH WATCHED IN HORROR as Babylonian soldiers set fire to the Temple in Jerusalem. His eyes burned from the smoke as well as his own grief, as he watched buildings throughout the city become pillaged and set ablaze. He wondered why the people had not listened to him. Why had they allowed themselves to be influenced by the pagan nations around them? If *only* the Jews would have heeded the prophets! If only they would have listened to Moses!

Gazing at the billowing black pillar of smoke rise, Jeremiah stared as the flames consumed the Holy Place. Although they were God's chosen people, the Jews slowly became like the Babylonians. Now, they had fallen under God's judgment, just as Moses predicted.

> But if you do not drive out the inhabitants of the land from before you, then it shall

> be that those whom you let remain shall be irritants in your eyes and *thorns in your sides*, and they shall harass you in the land where you dwell. Moreover it shall be that I will do to you as I thought to do to them—NUMBERS 33:55-56, ITALICS MINE.

A DEMONIC THORN

Any thorn will cause infection unless it is removed. A demonic thorn can prick the Church and cause infection, just as a splinter can inflame the skin and cause infection. The longer it is ignored, the greater the spread of infection. If neglected, the infection can spread and lead to amputation—or even worse, death.

To resolve the matter of a Jezebel spirit, God requires His servants to remove the demonic thorn that infects His Body. Godly confrontation is necessary in order for conviction and true repentance to occur.

Conviction and repentance occur with the help of the Holy Spirit. Pastors cannot force repentance upon anyone because we are *not* the "convicter" of sin. The Holy Spirit has that responsibility. We can pray that the Holy Spirit will convict an individual who operates with a Jezebel spirit. However, if an individual's behavior becomes obviously malicious and damaging to others in the church, a pastor must confront the issue. Decisive and unified action is needed by the pastor and the eldership before God takes action, as He was about to do with Thyatira.

RESPONSIBILITY FOR REMOVAL

Responsibility for addressing a Jezebel spirit belongs to the pastor. As an overseer of the flock, a pastor has the authority to confront and remove any troublesome person or problem in a church.

A pastor should not expect a prophet to address this issue. A prophet's responsibility is only to reveal an individual who covertly operates in a Jezebel spirit. Remember, the prophet Elijah ran from Jezebel. His successor, Elisha, realized that only kings had the authority to remove Jezebel. Thereby, God instructed Elisha to anoint Jehu to be king.

FIRST APPROACH

There are two basic approaches to take when confronting a Jezebelite. The first is to announce your conclusion (i.e., "you have a Jezebel spirit"), and then identify the reasons you drew that conclusion. However, this approach rarely works. The stigma of being called "Jezebel" is too offensive. In addition, such people have erroneously perceived that the Jezebel spirit is the Holy Spirit. Therefore, everything they have embraced becomes suspect. Since the Jezebel spirit counterfeits the Holy Spirit, they will have to admit that they were operating in the wrong spirit. They will need to acknowledge that the spirit which gave them comfort, power, insight, authority, value, and self-esteem is demonic. If they make such a confession, it will leave them feeling confused and disoriented, not knowing what to believe or who to trust.

For these reasons, I do not recommend taking this approach. More than likely, they will not acknowledge their problem. They will continue to believe they heard from the Holy Spirit. Consequently, they will begin to mount a defensive campaign against you, trying to entrench themselves further in the church so that you cannot get rid of them. Or, they will leave the church. While this solves your immediate problem, they remain unhealed. Pastors with a Kingdom mentality will grieve for the loss of God's original destiny for them.

SECOND APPROACH

The second and more apostolic approach is to identify and address core issues before announcing your conclusion. In fact, you may never have to identify that spirit to those who have it. Hopefully, they will see the issues and draw the conclusion on their own. For instance, if someone is spreading lies about you as pastor, you will need to confront the specific lie and discover why he or she has lied.

More than likely, this person has grown up with poor role models and has seen authority figures misuse their power. In a sense, this approach will require that the pastor help straighten out an individual's skewed thinking about authority figures. A pastor may want to encourage the individual to identify and sort through unrealistic expectations and re-parent himself or herself.

ADDRESS INDIVIDUAL'S FEARS

To encourage an individual to genuinely repent, a pastor will need to seek God's wisdom. He or she will also have to deal with the individual's fears.

Before people let you pray for them, they will need assurance that whatever made them vulnerable to operating with a Jezebel spirit will be eliminated. The door of access to this spirit of fear must be discovered, closed, sealed, and covered.

An individual must also feel safe around a pastor and others who are ministering to him or her. Love and wisdom must be clearly demonstrated in order for ministry to the Jezebelite to succeed. Simply having good intentions will not reassure the individual.

A myriad of fears may drive such an individual. It may be a fear of those in authority or a fear of those who are perceived as a threat. Discovering the root problem or access point that allowed this spirit to infiltrate will greatly facilitate the healing process. This will also help the person to refuse the same spirit in future situations. For example, if a Jezebel spirit has entered through a time when the person was feeling rejected, the specific situation that occurred should be identified. Then, the next time the individual is rejected—or perceives rejection—he or she will not resort to the old behavior of control and manipulation.

When you attempt to deliver Christians who have the Jezebel spirit, they will be afraid of losing everything. What you see as roots of the Jezebel spirit, they will see as necessary for their protection. They have mistakenly believed they are operating in the Holy Spirit. Therefore, they will believe that all their perceptions, opinions, words of knowledge, and dreams have come from God. The pastor's task is to dismantle this lie so that individuals can recognize the deception in which they have walked.

Normally, such people will need to be assured that God is at work to help them effectively resist and overcome a Jezebel spirit. Over time, this process of discernment and not yielding to old habits will build godly character. Remember: God is faithful to complete the healing that He has begun in their lives (Philippians 1:6).

REMORSE FOR GETTING CAUGHT

Remorse has underlying tones of regret for being caught. In addition, it suggests the possibility that the individual will repeat their actions again, at another time. It takes a seasoned leader to discern the difference between repentance and remorse.

Church discipline must continue until *true* repentance comes forth, evidenced by godly sorrow (2 Corinthians 7:10). Godly sorrow is a sign of a broken will. Even if an individual repents, he or she must not remain or be placed in *any* form of leadership. The individual's soul and spirit must first be renewed and restored. All of this takes time to heal properly. We must understand that this process involves more than forgiveness. It involves inner healing, which usually takes several years. Therefore, if the individual wants to start leading a small group, do not bow to their pressure. Rushing to reinstate him or her in leadership would be like sending a former alcoholic into a bar to witness. Wisdom cautions us not to do it!

WHEN PROBLEMS RESURFACE

Problems arise if the person denies having issues of control or manipulation. Surprisingly, denial often happens after a private meeting occurs in which the person admitted to having the problem. When these problems resurface, they will have a greater sting. Since you have already played your hand, the Jezebelite will begin to anticipate what you will say and craft clever rebuttals. Piece by piece, they will dismantle your entire case against them.

A pastor, who should have informed the leadership of the Jezebelite, will need to gather the leadership team. Together, the pastor and leaders will need to address and confront the individual quickly. Do not allow this problem to linger, because it will brew to hurricane strength. Repentance must be required immediately. (Please see the twelve steps outlined for pastors in Chapter 10.)

Since God requires two witnesses, you must have witnesses when confronting an individual with a Jezebel spirit. Furthermore, witnesses may be necessary if the individual later lies or twists what was said. By having witnesses present, you ensure that proper and necessary pastoral action will be taken. In addition, witnesses provide a power of agreement to bind and to loose. Together, you can bind the Jezebel spirit and its power from affecting future events in your church.

REMOVAL

If the individual is unrepentant and unwilling to undergo deliverance, he or she must be removed from the church. Scripture describes a man who challenged pastoral authority and who was severely corrected and removed from fellowship (1 Corinthians 5:4-5). These severe corrections require that leaders continue to demonstrate love, character, and valor.

RESTORATION

Because the apostle Paul was interested in the Kingdom and not in harboring a personal vendetta, several years after advising the removal of a man from the church in Corinth, he noticed the man's godly sorrow (2 Corinthians 2:4-11). The church leadership, however, had failed to notice it. So, Paul brought it to their attention and encouraged them to reinstate the man into church fellowship.

Likewise, after the individual has been removed, if the stronghold over the Jezebelite is truly broken, then we must forgive and restore the person to the church. Obviously, restoration must be done wisely by those who can accurately judge the individual's sincerity and depth of repentance.

TIME TO ACT

Jehu, who was the ruler of the longest-lived dynasty in Israel, was anointed king by Elisha and given a mandate by God to eliminate Jezebel and the house of Ahab (2 Kings 9:7). Jehu wasted no time in carrying out his assignment. At Jehu's command, Jezebel's own servants threw her down from her lofty perch on the city's wall. Her servants were eunuchs who did not yield to her seductions. As such, they were able to carry out Jehu's orders, in order that the true watchmen of God could stand there (2 Kings 9:33).

Likewise, a pastor who is going to confront Jezebel must become a spiritual eunuch. He or she must not be tempted by the lust of the flesh, the lust of the eyes, or the pride of life (1 John 2:16). Such a pastor must be as resolute and uncompromising as Jehu and as incapable of being seduced as Jezebel's eunuchs.

In this hour, I pray that godly pastors of kingly character, valor, and strength will arise. I pray that with courage, they will lay an axe at the root of this demonic spirit that seeks to destroy prophets, emasculate pastors, and pervert the Body of Christ. As God's people, we need to love what He loves and hate what He hates. We do not need to shrink back and become afraid of addressing and correcting lawlessness and rebellion that defile the Body of Christ.

THE ANTIDOTE TO LAWLESSNESS

Today, since lawlessness is a disease of our culture, I recommend that pastors take a proactive approach. They may want to consider having on-going teaching in a church on the topics of spiritual authority and lawlessness.

Chapter 12

Reclaiming Followers of Jezebel

There seemed to be nothing to do but to return to what he knew—fishing. For three years Peter had ministered beside Jesus. He had been included in His inner circle of disciples and been on the Mount of Transfiguration. In the end, however, Peter denied his Lord when it counted the most. Even though Peter was thrilled to see Jesus after the resurrection, he felt a sense of shame because of his denial. As Peter began to return to his old way of life, Jesus knew that Peter needed encouragement to embrace his calling. After breakfast by the seashore, Jesus asked Peter a series of questions designed to mend his broken spirit and restore him in the church (John 21:15-17).

Similarly, individuals who have been truly freed of a Jezebel spirit need to be encouraged and restored. They will need to be reminded that if we are faithful to confess our sins, the Lord is faithful to forgive us our sins and cleanse us from the effects of unrighteousness (1 John 1:9). Besides, what sin could be worse than Peter's three denials of Jesus at the most crucial moment in Jesus' life? Although He felt the sting of the betrayal from one of his closest friends, Jesus forgave and restored Peter.

No wounds are more painful in life than those we suffer at the hands of our friends, especially those whom we follow. These wounds will need to be touched by the Lord so that He can bring healing and wholeness. It makes no difference whether you are a pastor or a church member. All wounds from a Jezebel spirit must be healed.

Jesus anointed His Church to carry on the work of His Kingdom—healing the brokenhearted and setting free those who have been held captive by the wicked one (Isaiah 61:1). True healing comes when the following areas are addressed:

TEARING DOWN STRONGHOLDS

Ministry to a Jezebelite's followers will involve tearing down mental strongholds. In his book, *Healing the Nations*, John Sandford defines a mental stronghold as a practiced way of thinking that has become ingrained and automatic. It has a life and a will of its own. Strongholds are areas of the mind in which we are held captive and our perceptions are completely distorted.

For example, I once had a silly discussion with my wife over the color of flowers along the roadside. I saw them as coral flowers. My wife saw them as white flowers. I "knew" I was right, because of my perceptions. I could not understand why she kept insisting the flowers were white. It wasn't until I removed my yellow-tinted sunglasses that I realized my wife was right! The flowers were actually white. The tinted lens had distorted the flowers' color and caused them to appear coral. Because I thought I was right, I responded indignantly to my wife's protests with passionate conviction. This illustrates how strongholds can distort our perception of actual situations. In a similar way, we can interpret what happens through lenses that are tainted and distorted by our wounds.

As you walk-out your healing, you will need to bravely take a ruthless, personal assessment. It may be a shock to face reality and abandon your delusions. If we are to open the door to self-discovery and self-disclosure, we will need God's grace. As we open our hearts to the truth about ourselves, the healing journey begins.

The following areas may have allowed the enemy easy access to our lives and fueled the drive to follow someone with a Jezebel spirit.

1. An Emotional Dependency Toward Others

People who follow someone with a Jezebel spirit tend to be emotionally dependent. They have a great inner drive to be connected with someone or to have a special relationship with a particular person in order to heal their wounded self-esteem. While it is normal to need other people, overdependent people feel as though they need someone in their life all the time, fearing physical or emotional abandonment. Instead of developing healthy intimacy, they seek to enmesh and merge with another. Trying to fill the loneliness, emptiness, and lack of self-love has driven them into codependent and often abusive relationships.

God has placed deep within every human spirit a heart cry. He designed us to be relational people with a longing for fellowship. But unless we allow our heavenly Father to fill that core need, our identity will become like that of an orphan. We will drift along, desperately looking to others to meet our needs and adopt us.

For such wounded souls, God is the healing balm. God gently woos and draws us to the only place where our deep hunger can be satisfied. Our misplaced longings can *only* find true rest in God the Father. As the Holy Spirit bears witness that God is our Father, He will also attest that we are His children (Romans 8:16). We will be given a spirit of adoption, by which we are enabled to cry "Abba, Daddy!" To know Him as Father is to love and accept His authority over us. Our dependency then falls on Him, rather than on another person.

2. An Attitude of Fearfulness

Fear usually begins through unholy imagination. The mental aspect of our soul begins to focus on things that can potentially harm us. A spirit of fear then takes root in our soul.

Often those who follow someone with a Jezebel spirit have a history of enslaving fears of neglect, of rejection, of being punished, of loneliness, and perhaps of missing the will of God. These fears arise from our past experiences and are projected onto today's circumstances.

A spirit of fear is a sign of spiritual enslavement. It leads someone into being subservient to the control of others. Those who have followed a Jezebelite will have recurrent fears of being deceived again.They will be tempted to view authority as being tyrannical. All fears of being dominated or controlled must be brought to the Cross. Recent fears, as well as those rooted in childhood, must be reckoned as dead on the Cross (Romans 6:11) in order for new life to begin (2 Corinthians 5:17). Dying to these fears will free us to relate to others without fear.

To begin our healing, we must ask God to show us the circumstances that led to opening our soul to fear. We must—through faith—cast down what the Bible calls "vain imaginations." By faith, we need to cleanse ourselves of fear and ask other Christians who are free from fear to stand with us in agreement. We also need to ask God to fill us with love, power, and sound reasoning because His perfect love casts out our fear (1 John 4:18).

When our mind is ruled by our spirit, we will focus on the virtues that spring forth from the Lord. We will be able to concentrate on that which is true, noble, just, pure, lovely, of a good report, virtuous and praiseworthy (Philippians 4:8).

3. A Fear of Decision Making

When we relinquish our choices and decisions to another person, we run the risk of causing our spirit to atrophy. It will lose the ability to discern what is from God. We also risk falling into the sin of lawlessness (Hebrews 5:14).

God gives us our ability to exercise free will—the freedom to make choices and decisions. Without a will, we would be like Data, the android on Star Trek who only did whatever he was told. By giving us free will, God empowers us to follow through and complete the decisions we have made. Therefore, when we yield our will to another person, we have given that one the right to make decisions on our behalf. We then forfeit our ability to receive insight and revelation directly from God. In doing so, we have made Jezebel our idol, who now takes the place of God.

When we avoid making decisions, our motive may lie rooted in self-condemnation and a sense of incompetence. We may never have been taught how to make responsible decisions. Or, we may feel incapable of making good decisions. If that's the case, we may have been raised in a harsh and critical home where punishments for making mistakes outweighed the actual offenses. Hence, it seemed as if we could never do anything good enough! So, we avoid making decisions due to the fear of being penalized for making bad ones. To compensate, we acquire a mind-set that anticipates failure. We become afraid to take risks. Instead, we listen to the whispers in our head that predict eventual failure. Shying away from responsibility, we then grow up unable, indifferent, unmotivated, or disinterested in making decisions.

To overcome a fear of failure, we will need to change how we think. We will need to learn how to envision success, *not* failure. The healthier we become, the more we will be able to practice making good decisions. Remember, God is faithful to show His will to any who humbly seek Him and are willing to obey His will.

4. A Deep Sense of Shame

Shame is the sense of feeling fundamentally bad, inadequate, defective, unworthy, or not measuring up to standards. Many need healing from a deep sense of shame.

At some point in our life, all of us feel shame. But for those who have followed Jezebel, shame will be a constant painful memory. They will doubt their ability to hear from God, as though they are eternally flawed or blemished. They may believe that God is disgusted with them. Therefore, it may be helpful to remind them that all is *not* lost. Instead, a great lesson has been learned.

It's often at our lowest point that we discover the wonder of God's amazing and profound grace. Grace is contrary to shame. While shame brings depression, grace brings hope and lightheartedness.

Grace refers to God's undeserved kindness directed toward us. It is unearned and unrepayable. Through God's grace, we are able to bond with our loving heavenly Father who longs to lavish His great love upon us. As we embrace His Son Jesus, who is the atoning sacrifice for our sins, He calls us His "sons and daughters." When we journey through the "dark night of the soul," we may be able to hear God whisper to us, "I love and accept you. The plans I have for you are for good and not for evil" (Jeremiah 29:11).

5. A Fear of Trusting Again

Whenever we appeal to another person for our spiritual strength, our heart turns away from the Lord. We have allowed the other person to be our source of strength.

Scripture admonishes us to place our trust in the Lord (Psalm 37:3; Psalm 71:5; Proverbs 3:5; Isaiah 50:10). Personally, I do this by quieting my heart and looking to God. Knowing that I belong to Him helps me to trust and obey His will for my life. Knowing what He wants me to do, moment by moment, is a daily quest. God calls us to live our faith by trusting in Him. Prayer helps me to wait on God for His direction instead of acting impulsively in my own self-interests. When we put our trust in God, He enables us to trust the spiritual authority that He has placed in our lives (1 Peter 2:13-3:6; 5:5-6).

Bonding with God is the basis for rebuilding relationships with others. The stronger our bond with God, the greater our ability to form healthy relationships with others. Our courage to trust again flows from our connectedness with God.

While Jesus touched many people, He only disclosed His heart to a few close friends who were committed to Him. Likewise, we should only trust another individual to the degree that we see Jesus rather than a religious pretense, manifested in their life (Micah 7:5-13).

6. The Consequences of Naiveté

Naiveté can place a person at great risk. Naiveté implies that an individual is simple-minded, ignorant, foolish, and able to be ensnared and mislead (Proverbs 27:12). Such people are gullible and are often exploited by the Jezebelite. Those who are controlling and manipulative will instinctively sniff out an opportunity to take advantage of them.

Naiveté can also foster our need to idolize another individual. Whenever we feel an excessive admiration toward someone, we will begin to form unrealistic expectations of them. We will exaggerate their good points and become blinded to their faults. This unhealthy esteem and affection actually hinders, rather than edifies, the idolater.

Throughout Scripture, we are encouraged to embrace wisdom, knowledge, and discretion which preserve our life and protect us from evil (Proverbs 2:10-13). Our being wise and discrete will repel those who seek to oppress and dominate us.

It is never too late to learn godly wisdom, discretion, and discernment. No matter how many mistakes may lie in your past, God's mercies are new every morning

(Lamentations 3:22-23). His ability to forgive is greater than our ability to fail.

7. A Loss of Joy and Innocence

A loss of joy will be evident in the life of someone who is recovering from the pain of following a Jezebelite. The followers' withered souls will make it difficult for them to express their emotions. They may begin to slide into a dark depression. As they begin more and more to embrace God's grace, their joy will return, bringing strength.

God has created us to be *full* of joy. Knowing Him intimately brings joy, which enriches our life. I have discovered that joy is like a fountain of youth. It prevents, alleviates, and cures the diseases of our soul (Proverbs 17:22). Joy gives us spiritual vitality. Experiencing joy also empowers us to cultivate healthy relationships with others (Nehemiah 8:10).

Walking in a deep, abiding sense of joy requires childlike innocence. Innocence allows us to embrace simple faith that looks to our loving heavenly Father to solve all of our dilemmas. In time, as our relationship with the Lord deepens, our spontaneity and childlike innocence will be restored. As we let go of trying to control others, we will stop trying to predict what others will do, and thereby, rediscover a childlike wonder and innocence.

8. Fearing the Supernatural

Those who have been wounded by a Jezebelite may fear anything that hints of the supernatural or of the spiritual realm. This fear will come as an overreaction to having been deceived initially. Thus, a thick wall of protection is erected in their soul to guard against further deception.

Sadly, this overreaction will hinder a wounded follower from appreciating the endless variety of God's supernatural gifts such as dreams and visions. They may regard anything beyond their five senses as being suspicious. They may feel uncomfortable during a worship service when God's presence is powerfully manifested. However, this reaction will only cause them to hold God at arm's length.

Did you realize that supernatural gifts are actually tools by which we attack the enemy's camp? It's true! By disdaining such supernatural gifts, we inadvertently play into the enemy's plans and we revert back to the old adage, "What we don't know can't harm us."

Our ability to embrace supernatural gifts is founded on knowing God as our loving heavenly Father. As a Father, God yearns to give good gifts to His children. When God manifests His presence supernaturally, we see His awesome glory and majestic splendor. He is truly a God like no other! He is a living God who dwells among an innumerable company of supernatural beings (Hebrews 12:22-24).

9. Believing a Lie

Unfortunately, many followers of a Jezebelite have been deceived by demons, and thereby, blinded to the demonic grip that ensnares them. They have formerly viewed others—even pastors—as being deceived and demonically influenced. They will see themselves as being an elite spiritual force, immune to demonic attack. Sadly, those entangled by the web of deception will erroneously look to the Jezebelite, instead of the Lord, as a fortress of protection against the demonic realm.

Trusting in evil spirits—whether you know them to be evil spirits or not—places you under their authority and false protection. Thus, you have given these spirits keys to your life. Since they provide a harmful authority, you will need deliverance from their domain. If you have an aversion to deliverance, ask God to remove any stronghold that you may have and that blinds you to seeing the answer to your healing.

10. Telling Other Voices to Stop

For a season, demonic spirits will test former followers to see if they really mean business. These people will need to command the voices and masters in their mind to cease instructing or beguiling them. If these seductive spirits return to tempt them, they need to resist them.

From now on, they are free to follow no other voice but the voice of Jesus. They need to embrace the words of Jesus, "My sheep hear My voice...I know them, and they follow Me" (John 10:27).

11. Refusing a Jezebelite's Influence

Former followers should not receive the counsel, prayers, or the laying on of hands from anyone whom they sense operates with a Jezebel spirit. It may be wise for them to consider getting rid of any personal items—clothing, jewelry, books, music, art, knick-knacks or photos—that have been given by the Jezebelite. These items can represent soul ties that will hinder their journey to freedom. They may want to ask the Lord if they need to destroy such items (Deuteronomy 26; Acts 19:19).

12. RECONCILING WITH FAMILY AND FRIENDS

> Therefore if you bring your gift to the altar, and there remember that your brother has something against you, leave your gift there before the altar, and go your way. First be reconciled to your brother, and then come and offer your gift—MATTHEW 5:23-24.

While operating under the stronghold of a Jezebel spirit, it is easy for us to become blinded to the wounds we have inflicted on others. Ask the Lord to help you recognize your actions and to see them through other people's eyes. This will open your eyes as to how your manipulation and control brought injury to others.

Forgiveness does not mean excusing someone's behavior. Rather it acknowledges the actual offense and then chooses not to hold that offense against the person. When Jesus Christ died on the Cross, His blood was the payment for our sins so that we could be truly forgiven. Likewise by extending forgiveness to someone, we mirror the depth of God's forgiveness to us.

> Let all bitterness, wrath, anger, clamor, and evil speaking be put away from you, with all malice. And be kind to one another, tenderhearted, forgiving one another, even as God in Christ forgave you—EPHESIANS 4:31-32.

Followers of a Jezebelite will need to ask forgiveness of individuals they have wronged or hurt, and leaders whose church or ministry they have maligned. They may want to ask God to help in making their confession. They may want to communicate that they realize their actions were intolerable. As they feel some of the pain they inflicted on someone, they will be able to ask sorrowfully for the person's forgiveness.

Former followers may feel compelled to make amends with their loved ones. Such reconciliation will bring about restoration and greater spiritual release. As a result, curses spoken by the spirit of Jezebel are rendered void and powerless.

The process of forgiveness will take time. They will need time to recuperate and reenter old routines. Family chores that have been left undone will need to be resumed, not begrudgingly but in an attitude of gratefulness. This kindness will help restore healthy relationships. Godly counselors can also be beneficial in the healing process.

13. Creating Healthy Relationships

The energy needed to initiate new relationships may be hampered by lethargy, which comes as a by-product of being dominated by another person. Walking through the process of healing will be tiring. Former followers of a Jezebelite may feel exhausted physically and emotionally. At the same time, they will need to be encouraged to participate in church activities and not to isolate from others. They will need to be motivated to embrace self-discipline and to establish healthy boundaries with others. In this way, they will recapture a Holy Spirit-led will.

14. Embrace True Humility

Humility and obedience always lead us to God. They open a door for God's grace to be extended to us. True repentance is the ultimate act of humility. We know that "God resists the proud, but gives grace to the humble" (James 4:6). Each day, we need to ask the Holy Spirit to convict us, so that any hurtful or harmful thing in our life is exposed. Then, we should come to our heavenly Father and to one another with godly sorrow. True repentance will always set us free from bondage.

15. Trust Jesus Daily

When our needs for love go unmet, codependency and the impulse to "bend into" another person is bred. Instead of looking to another person who is limited and unreliable, we need to develop our spiritual well-being. Each day, we need to look to Jesus, who is sufficient to supply all our needs—emotional, physical, spiritual, and relational. He is the all-sufficient One! In Him resides the fullness of abundant life (John 1:4).

> Trust in the Lord with all your heart, and lean not on your own understanding; in all your ways acknowledge Him, and He shall direct your paths—PROVERBS 3:5-6.

16. Cleansing Prayer

Former followers of a Jezebelite may want to pray these words of repentance and deliverance along the journey toward wholeness:

"Heavenly Father, I need Your Holy Spirit to help me *not* think and live according to my old ways. I place my childhood fears and bloodline curses behind me and ask You to cancel them. By faith in the Lord Jesus Christ, I choose not to be enslaved to them any longer!

"Today, I lay aside my fear of facing the pain from past friendships, romances, lovers, and relatives. I renounce the spirits of pride, bitterness, lying, self-exaltation, rebellion, witchcraft, and the occult. I choose to *not* walk in these any longer. When I am tested by these deceiving spirits, I want to respond in godliness. God, please remove any mental strongholds and to help me think and see clearly.

"I choose *not* to listen to other spiritual voices. Instead, I choose to listen to Your voice. From this time forth, I will *not* trust in lying spirits nor the spirits who claim to offer me protection from evil. I close every door to Satan. I will *not* seek a false defense to shield myself from wrong, exploitation, or harm. I look to You, Lord Jesus and place my trust in You to protect me from the harm of well-meaning people and from demonic spirits. Jesus, I choose You to be my Savior and Holy Spirit, I choose You to be my defender. "Lord Jesus Christ, please forgive my sins. I confess that I have *not* loved rightly. I have resented others. I now recognize this as sin and confess this to you now.

I choose to forgive those who have hurt me. By Your blood, I forgive myself as You have forgiven me. I am sorry for my sins. I confess and renounce them, known and unknown. I believe you died on the Cross for my sins, and that you rose from the dead and ascended to God the Father. You now sit at His right hand. With repentance in my heart, I ask You, Lord, to deliver me from the snare of the fowler and to set me free. Your truth is a shield to me. Under Your wings, I seek refuge.

"Lord Jesus, I claim Your promise in Psalm 91:14-15: Because I have set my love upon You, You will deliver me. You will set me on high because I have known Your Name. I will call upon You, and You will answer me. You will be with me in trouble. You will deliver me and honor me."

IN SUMMARY

It is my prayer that those who have been cleansed and healed of the Jezebel spirit and its influence will become strong in the Lord Jesus Christ and go forth to build the Kingdom of God. May the Lord's wisdom greatly increase in His Church, and may He grant us the ability to minister restoration to one another.

As the Holy Spirit is being poured out upon the Lord's menservants and maidservants in these last days (Acts 2:18), may God-breathed prophesy, signs, and wonders arise and transform our generation. May His Kingdom come, may His will be done on Earth as it is in Heaven!

APPENDIX A

14 CHARACTERISTICS OF THE JEZEBEL SPIRIT

HERE ARE SOME OF the characteristics that accompany the work of the Jezebel spirit. Please keep in mind that a person heavily influenced by this demonic spirit may do many of the following, at one time or another, although not necessarily in the order described. Furthermore, a single characteristic does not indicate that someone has a "full-blown" Jezebel spirit. It may simply mean that the person is still spiritually and emotionally immature. When a combination of several of the fourteen characteristics exists, however, there is a strong indication that an individual is influenced by a Jezebel spirit. Also remember that one characteristic may be clearly noticeable, but other traits may be hidden and yet profound. A prolonged manifestation of any of these traits warrants a closer look at the individual and the situation.

1. While it's almost unrecognizable at first, such individuals are threatened by a prophetic leader, who is the main target of concern. Although such people will seem to have prophetic gifts, their aim is to actually control those who move in the prophetic realm.

2. To increase their favor, such individuals often zero in on a pastor and church staff, and then seek to find the weakest link in order to subdue them. Their eventual goal is to run the church.

3. Seeking to gain popular and pastoral endorsement, such individuals will form strategic affiliations with people who are perceived by others to be spiritual or influential with others.

4. To appear spiritual, such individuals will seek recognition by manipulating situations to gain an advantage. Such individuals often conjure up dreams and visions from their imaginations, or they borrow them from others.

5. When these individuals receive initial recognition, they often respond with false humility. However, this trait is short-lived.

6. When confronted, these individuals will become defensive. They will justify their actions with phrases like, "I'm just following God" or "God told me to do this."

7. These individuals will often allege having great spiritual insight into church government and affairs, but they will not appeal to proper authority. Rather they *first* appeal to others. Often their opinion becomes the "last word" on matters, thereby elevating their thoughts above the pastor's.

8. Having impure motives, these individuals will seek out others, desiring to have "disciples," needing constant affirmation from their followers.

9. Desiring to avoid accountability, these individuals prefer to pray for people in isolated situations—in a corner or in another room. Thus, innuendoes and false "prophetic" words cannot be easily challenged.

10. Eager to gain control, these people will gather others and seek to teach them. While the teachings may begin correctly, "doctrine" is often established that is not supported by the Word of God.

11. Deceiving others by soulish prophecy or by giving words that someone wants to hear, these individuals seek to gain credibility. They prophesy half-truths or little known facts, as though they were from God. Such individuals may also take advantage of someone else's poor memory by twisting their previous prophecies to make it seem as if their words have come to pass.

12. Although the "laying on of hands" is biblical, these individuals like to impart a higher level in the spirit—or break down walls that have held someone back—by the "laying on of hands." However, their touch is actually a curse. Instead of a holy blessing, an evil spirit may be imparted.

13. Masking poor self-esteem with spiritual pride, these individuals want to be seen as the most spiritual ones in the church. They may be the first to cry, wail, or mourn—claiming a burden from God. However, they are no different from the Pharisees who announced their gifts in order to be seen by men.

14. Usually such individual's family life is shaky. These individuals may be single or married. If married, their spouse is usually weak spiritually, unsaved, or miserable. They begin to dominate and control everyone in the family.

APPENDIX B

FUNDAMENTALS OF STRONGHOLDS

A stronghold is an area of the mind where darkness reigns. It is a system of logic, rooted in a lie, that an individual has come to accept. This system of thought is formed behind any habitual response, addiction, fixation, compulsion, obsession, and/or inordinate fear.

As such, a stronghold is *any* thought pattern alien to the Word of God. It serves as a mental or emotional "command post" to which the enemy has access. This mental or emotional word or thought system is designed to create misinformation and thereby affect an individual's decision-making ability. Consequently, a stronghold keeps a person from embracing true Christlikeness.

I have listed some fundamental truths about how strongholds operate and hold people captive:

1. Strongholds are a primary strategy of Satan's work around the world and in our lives.
2. Strongholds form presuppositions that distort our perceptions of everything we encounter.
3. Everyone has strongholds in their lives.
4. None of us are as free as Jesus' death on the Cross was purposed to make us. Remember, the blood of Jesus cleanses us from *all* sin (1 John 1:7). His blood is a weapon that disables strongholds.
5. As my friend Jack Taylor says, "If you are as free as you want to be, then you are as free as you're going to be—until your desire changes."

STRONGHOLDS IN OPERATION

1. Strongholds prevent or retard our emotional and spiritual growth and maturity.
2. Strongholds cause conflict, separation, and divorce in marriage. In the church, strongholds cause division. They provoke bitterness, jealousy, anxiety, and depression.
3. Strongholds empower Satan and his demons, while grieving the Holy Spirit and God's angels.
4. Strongholds keep individuals from accepting what Christ has made them to be and thus keeps them from fulfilling their personal destiny in God.
5. Strongholds are a foothold or a place of operation that the devil possesses in us (Ephesians 4:22).
6. Strongholds produce financial disorder and will bring about spiritual disorientation.

7. Strongholds weaken our body and make us vulnerable to diseases.
8. Strongholds provoke us to respond to others in ways that even we do not understand. They fragment attempted friendships and steal our joy and hope.
9. Strongholds stifle our faith and distort Scripture. They cloud and darken our minds and imprison our spirit.
10. Strongholds can only be killed at the root. They cannot be removed simply by addressing the manifestation.
11. Strongholds allow us to give only a begrudging love, at best. They keep us from forgiving others.

MY PRAYER

Here's a prayer that I offer every day for my family and myself. Feel free to adapt it to your daily devotion with the Lord:

> Lord, I humbly admit that I have mental strongholds in my life. These strongholds distort my perception of what You are doing. I ask You to tear down these strongholds so that I can perceive clearly.
>
> Today, I loose myself in the Holy Spirit and to walk in the fullness of Your purpose for my life. I know that I am capable of doing much more in You than I allow to happen. Therefore, I loose my spirit, soul, and body to be *totally* yours today! Amen.

APPENDIX C

AMY'S STORY

THE FOLLOWING STORY IS a true account of a woman who followed someone with a Jezebel spirit. It is my prayer that her testimony will be an encouragement to those who have succumbed to this spirit. I pray that her story will be prayerfully considered. May Amy's testimony shine the way to true freedom for those who are called to bear the testimony of Jesus, which is the spirit of prophecy.

AMY'S STORY

My first encounter with a Jezebel spirit began several years ago. I had gone forward for prayer following a worship service at church. I desperately needed physical and emotional healing. For several years, I had been to many specialists and psychiatrists, but they never seemed to help. I was exhausted and at the end of my rope. After prayer, a woman near the front of the church approached me. She seemed eager to help and sounded very spiritual. She asked for my telephone number and expressed an interest in calling me. Although I had no idea why, I gave her my phone number.

When the woman called, I told her about an inner voice that seemed clear, distinct, and almost audible. It would teach me something in the Bible and told me about my condition and how to become free. She said that she, too, had heard its voice. She seemed like a godly woman, an intercessor, and seemed to know a great deal about the Bible. I began to trust her.

THE TEACHING

We started studying the Bible and pursuing revelation together. She insisted that I could deliver myself through Scripture. She emphasized deliverance. She was always "pro-God," but very subtly, Jesus was never mentioned. She said that we—not Jesus—were the mediators between God and man. We began using the names of God to deliver ourselves. Thereby, we were supposedly learning a newfound freedom in the spirit. Although I desperately wanted to escape my emotional pain, I spent four years delivering myself from one thing after another—or in her lingo: "taking back the land."

Looking good to this woman became very important to me. Later, I realized that she fed off my spirit and my adulation of her. She began to stress spiritual disciplines such as fasting. I would fast to receive her approval, as well as God's. At first, the two of us seemed to be on a journey together. If I learned something, I would tell her and she would respond. If she learned something, she would tell me and I would do it. Then, we compiled our thoughts into a teaching on deliverance. If someone had problems with a particular spirit, we would offer to minister to him or her.

Amy's Marriage Deteriorated

As our relationship developed, my relationship with my husband deteriorated. He planned to leave me. I thought that he was the problem. I was blind to seeing my errors. This woman only made my marriage problems worse. Whenever she came to my home, she showed little respect for my husband's feelings. If he came home while we were visiting, she would overstay her visit and tie up my time. My husband, who worked two jobs, wanted time to relax and be with his family. My friend was thoughtless, rude, and insensitive to my husband and my family.

A Guise of Submission

I thought I was submissive to my husband because I was compliant with certain things. But to be honest, I was not a submissive wife. I was still calling the shots and getting my way. If I didn't get my way, I would continually voice my displeasure. Tension continued to mount in my marriage. Although it's easy to talk about submission, it's difficult to live it out daily.

Clothing Given, Dreams Received

When a new pastor joined our church, he spoke on the Jezebel spirit. Presumptively, my friend and I decided that he was a false prophet. I even had a dream that he had a Jezebel spirit! So, I decided to counsel him about getting some deliverance. I worked up some notes and gave them to this pastor. He politely took them without saying much. After that, my friend and I thought he was okay. We even took pride that he "received" my teaching. However, he knew how to detect a Jezebel spirit and he was quickly clued into both of us.

CONVICTION

Four years later someone exposed my prideful deception. My husband had become a Christian during that time. One evening, my sister and her husband, along with another couple, prayed for me and my husband. I could tell my sister was hesitant. But as soon as she began to speak, I began to weep.

She said I had a spirit of deception and that my friend had a Jezebel spirit. At first, I heard a roar in my ears. "This can't be true," I thought. Horrified, I kept quiet. But then, another quieter voice that seemed to come from my heart like a whisper said, "Receive this, it is true." As I did, the other voice left.

When I got home, I threw all my notes and teachings into the garbage. Then, I went to my closet and pulled out clothes that she had given me. I separated myself from this woman for months. During that time, I was hurting and still questioned if the revelation were true. Some days, I was tempted to deny what my sister had said. I thought I had understood the Jezebel spirit and had even delivered myself of that spirit. Even though I had done much to distance myself from this spirit, it seemed as though it was still inside my mind and my body.

Parting

In retrospect, I think I was fearful. My thoughts were full of anxiety and insecurity. I thought that I needed this woman to lean on—not realizing that the Lord had given my husband to me to serve that purpose. All along, the Lord warned me of this woman, but I had not broken off the relationship. I cannot blame my friend for what was inside of me. I cannot blame her for the voice I heard. Looking back, I realize that I had heard this voice before I ever met her. But the voice and the thoughts inside of me became more prominent when I joined forces with her.

Separating from this woman was like losing my mother. For years, I had fed off her spirit and vice versa. Sadly, after all those years, I had no real spiritual fruit or supernatural power. Thinking I was wise, I discovered that I had lived a life of deceit and rebellion.

Hungry for Mysteries

I had hungered to know the great mysteries of God. Then, the Lord said to me softly, "You sought to know all knowledge and all mysteries about Me, but the greatest mystery is that while you were yet a sinner, Christ died for you." It was a powerful and humble revelation for me.

A Revealing Dream

Shortly thereafter, the Lord gave me a dream. My husband and two sons were on a hay wagon. I started to climb into the wagon, but my husband said, "Who is going to push the wagon?" Filled with anger and resentment, I climbed off the wagon. "I have been working all day long, and now I have to push this wagon home," I complained. But surprisingly, when I began to push the wagon, it wasn't a hard thing to do. It was really light. Still, I could not understand why my husband wouldn't help me.

When I told the dream to my pastor, I said, "Sometimes with my husband, I feel like I'm talking to a wall!" My pastor graciously encouraged me to pray the passage in Ephesians 5 so that my husband would come into his rightful position.

As soon as I got home, I got on my knees. "God, I've gone through four years of doing what I thought was holy. I thought that I knew how to pray, but I realize that I do not." As I was saying those words, I remembered my dream. Suddenly I saw a vision of myself climbing onto the wagon. My two sons had full rein. I said nothing. I stopped telling everyone what to do and where they should be. Instead, I was riding along on the wagon! Then, I saw my husband get off the wagon.

The Lord spoke to me very clearly, "The wall you've sensed in your husband was not because your husband was unwilling to push, but because you were unwilling to let him push." With great mercy, God showed me that I was the wall in the relationship with my husband. I had not allowed my husband to hear from God for himself. I realized my attitude had been, "God, you tell me, and then I'll tell my husband." I quickly repented for my prideful heart.

ASKING FORGIVENESS

I had one final thing to do. The Lord dealt with me about what I had taught. I was grieved about misleading people. The Lord told me, "You're going to have to ask their forgiveness for what you've shared with others." I had shared the teachings and revelations of Jezebel with others.

The Holy Spirit prompted me to listen to my pastor's teaching tape on the Jezebel spirit. I was deeply convicted by the reference in Revelation to "those who do not hold to this teaching." I realized that I had held onto the teaching of this demonic spirit, and shared it with others. The passage revealed God's judgment for Jezebel and her followers. My spirit was deeply grieved.

At that time, God granted me a deep repentance. I confessed to God, "The voice which I received was not Your voice. The teaching was not Your teaching." That night, I engaged in spiritual warfare. I confessed to God: "This teaching that I have believed was from Satan." The next morning, the light dawned and my testimony became apparent. I shared it with my pastor.

He told me that a year earlier he had seen me sitting in the woman's car. He sensed that we were involved with this spirit. He wanted to tell me, but the Lord would not allow him. He knew that I would simply react in rebellion. He had godly wisdom to wait until the God-appointed time.

KEYS TO FORGIVENESS AND HUMILITY

It should be easy to forgive someone. Since I have been forgiven much, I need to love much. And yet, I was in such pain. Why was I still holding on to my anger and resentment? The Lord Jesus says to cast our burdens and cares upon Him. But I guess that I hadn't really cast them upon Him, until now. I humbled myself before my husband and asked his forgiveness. "I've made so many mistakes in trying to lead our family. But I need to show grace to let you lead us."

In times past, I would not trust my husband's decisions unless I had a part in making them. Today, I am learning to trust my husband just as I trust God. I have chosen to be submissive to him according to Ephesians 5:22, and to love the Lord Jesus Christ and Him only.

The Jezebel spirit has a pretense of exalting God, but it always exalts self. This spirit almost destroyed my marriage as well as my life. I have seen that spirit do the same to other women and their families.

RECOMMENDED READING

Barclay, Mark T. *The Sin of Lawlessness: A Lethal Practice.* Midland, MI: Mark T. Barclay Publication, 1989.

Berry, Carmen Renee, M.S.W. and Mark W. Baker, Ph.D. *Who's to Blame?* Colorado Springs: Pinion Press, 1996.

Carter, Les, Ph.D. and Frank Minirth, M.D. *The Anger Workbook*. Nashville: Thomas Nelson, Inc., 1993.

Devenish, David. *Demolishing Strongholds*. Milton Keynes, England: Word Publishing, 2000.

Gibson, Noel and Phyl. *Deliver Our Children From the Evil One*. Kent, U.K.: Sovereign World, Ltd., 1992.

—— *Evicting Demonic Intruders.* Chichester, U.K.: New Wine Press, 1993.

Godwin, Rick. *Exposing Witchcraft in the Church*. Orlando: Creation House, 1997.

Groom, Nancy. *From Bondage to Bonding: Escaping Codependency, Embracing Biblical Love.* Colorado Springs: NavPress, 1991.

—— *Heart to Heart About Men: Words of Encouragement for Women of Integrity.* Colorado Springs: NavPress, 1995.

Joyner, Rick. *Epic Battles of the Last Days*. New Kensington, PA: Whitaker House, 1995.

Ketterman, Grace, M.D. and David Hazard. *When You Can't Say "I Forgive You": Breaking the Bonds of Anger and Hurt.* Colorado Springs: NavPress, 2000.

Malone, Henry. *Shadow Boxing.* Irving, TX: Truth Publishing, 1999.

Mellody, Pia. *Facing Love Addiction: Giving Yourself the Power to Change the Way You Love.* San Francisco: HarperCollins Publishers, 1992.

Moore, John L. *The Limits of Mercy*. Nashville: Thomas Nelson, Inc., 1996.

Myer, Joyce. *Managing Your Emotions Instead of Your Emotions Managing You!* Tulsa, OK: Harrison House, 1997.

Payne, Leanne. *The Broken Image: Restoring Personal Wholeness Through Healing Prayer.* Wheaton: Crossway Books, 1981.

Sandford, John. *Healing the Nations: A Call to Global Intercession.* Grand Rapids: Chosen Books, a division of Baker Book House, 2000.

Sandford, John and Mark. *A Comprehensive Guide to Deliverance and Inner Healing.* Grand Rapids: Fleming H. Revell, a division of Baker Book House Company, 1992.

Sandford, John and R. Loren Sandford. *The Renewal of the Mind.* Tulsa: Victory House Publishers, 1991.

Schaumburg, Harry W., Dr. *False Intimacy: Understanding the Struggle of Sexual Addiction.* Colorado Springs: NavPress, 1997.

Smith, Eddie and Alice. *Intercessors and Pastors: The Emerging Partnership of Watchmen and Gatekeepers.* Houston: SpiriTruth Publishing, 2000.

Whiteman, Tom Ph.D. and Randy Petersen *Victim of Love: How You Can Break the Cycle of Bad Relationships.* Colorado Springs: Pinion Press, 1998.

ABOUT THE AUTHOR

JOHN PAUL JACKSON HAS been at the forefront of prophetic ministry for more than twenty years. He has authored several books, produced multiple worship recordings, published a magazine, and has appeared on television broadcasts such as *The 700 Club*, Benny Hinn's *This Is Your Day* broadcast, TBN's *Praise the Lord* broadcast, Cornerstone Television, Daystar Television, and God Digital.

It was his great love for the Body of Christ that prompted John Paul in 1993 to launch Streams Ministries International, a non-profit organization that endeavors to encourage, motivate, and equip individuals to walk in greater maturity, wisdom, character, and holiness. As founder and chairman, John Paul travels extensively around the world teaching on the art of hearing God, dreams and visions, and revelatory gifts. As people experience the supernatural power of God in his meetings, lives continue to be transformed.

John Paul and his wife, Diane, have two children and three grandchildren.

I AM: 365 Names of God

Designed for daily reading and meditation,
John Paul Jackson has collected 365 names of God that
will guide you into becoming a person who
consistently abides in God's presence. Hardback.

Retail $24

I AM: Inheriting the Fullness of God's Names

As you embark on the glorious adventure of knowing God,
let Him show you the amazing mysteries and wonders
revealed for those who bear His name.

Retail $10

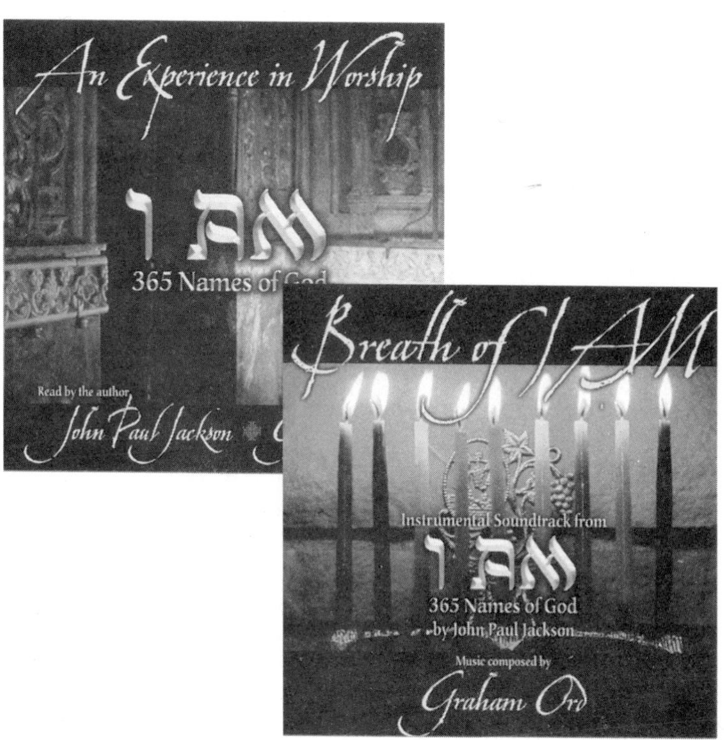

I AM: 365 Names of God CD

Listen as John Paul Jackson reads the names of God from his book. Experience the peace, comfort, healing, provision, and transforming power that comes from meditating on God's names.

Retail $16

Breath of I AM CD

Ideal for times of meditation, prayer, and therapeutic healing, this soothing instrumental creates an atmosphere that will soothe your spirit and calm your soul.

Retail $16

UNDERSTANDING DREAMS AND VISIONS

Explore the world of dreams. Unravel the mysteries of dream interpretation in this inspiring series and discover how to apply God-given insights in your waking life. You don't want to miss these fascinating insights from a gifted dream expert.

(Six-CD set)

RETAIL $42

Keys to Receiving God's Justice

Have you been attacked, robbed, or cheated by the enemy? Implement God's plan of justice in your life to avenge the enemy's attacks. Insure that you and your family receive every blessing stolen from your generational line.

(*One-CD set*)

Retail $8

MAXIMIZING HEAVEN'S HELP

Understand how to activate God's angels in your life. Discover how to change destructive cycles. Learn how to position yourself to unleash your full potential.

(Four-CD set)

RETAIL $27

ADVANCING TO THE NEXT SPIRITUAL LEVEL

Go higher! Live in the power of God's glory, presence, and unfathomable deity. Become a victorious champion, conquering colossal giants and inheriting all of God's promises and blessings. Get ready to advance to your full potential.

(Four-CD set)

RETAIL $27

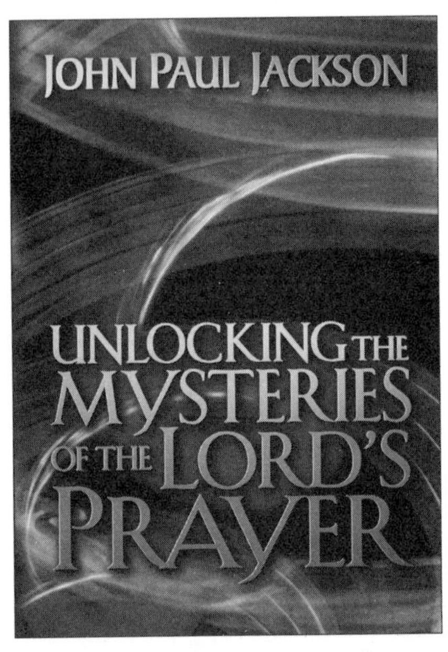

Unlocking the Mysteries of the Lord's Prayer

Are you hungry for a deeper revelation of prayer? Uncover seven dimensions of the Lord's prayer and grasp essential keys that open the doors of Heaven.

(Four-CD set)

Retail $27

True Spirituality

at is True Spirituality? How can you tell the difference between ***True*** and ***rk*** Spirituality? In this two-disc set, John Paul discusses how the gurus of day can call themselves spiritual and in some ways actually be correct in doing so. Learn how to avoid the subtle persuasions of the enemy by following the One, True, Pure, Holy Spirit.

(Two-CD set)

Retail $24.00

7 Days Behind the Veil - Hardcover

If you could stand before the throne of God, what would it be like? Do you think it would change you? Join John Paul Jackson as he describes what it like to love God from Heaven's throne room, touching what you've only dreamed about-and suddenly discovering that your dreams were far too small.

Retail $10.00

Order Form

- Order Online: **www.streamsministries.com**
- Call toll-free (U.S. and Canada): **1.888.441.8080**
- Postal orders: **Streams Ministries, 4004 Gateway Dr. Ste 100 Colleyville, TX 76034**

Quantity	Title	Price
______	______________________________	______
______	______________________________	______
______	______________________________	______
______	______________________________	______

Domestic Shipping and Handling Charges

Up to $20	$5.00
$20 01 to $50.00	$7.00
$50.01 to $75.00	$8.00
$75.01 to $100.00	$9.00
More than $100	10% of Subtotal

SubTotal ________

Shipping and Handling ________

Total This Order ________

For AK, HI, PR, USVI, Canada, or Mexico, please double the shipping charges.

International Rates: All international orders must be paid by credit card only. Please specify international surface or airmail shipping. The shipping cost will be added to your credit card charges.

(Please print clearly)

Name: ______________________________

Street Address: ______________________________

Apt. ______________ City: ______________

State: ______________ Zip: ______________

Country: ______________ Phone: ______________

E-Mail: ______________________________

Method of Payment:

___ Check or Money Order (Make check payable to *Streams Ministries)*

___ Credit Card: ❑ Visa ❑ MasterCard ❑ American Express ❑ Discover

Card number: ______-______-______-______ Expiration Date: ____/_____

Card Holder (please print): ______________________________

Signature: ______________________________

(Credit card orders cannot be processed without signature)